I0326642

LIVING THE LAPTOP LIFESTYLE
HOW TO START & GROW
A PROFITABLE ONLINE BUSINESS
SO YOU CAN QUIT YOUR JOB
LIVING THE LAPTOP LIFESTYLE

LIVING THE LAPTOP LIFESTYLE:

How to Start & Grow a Profitable Online Business So You Can Quit Your Job.

Published in Australia by

Cheriton House Publishing Pty Ltd

Brisbane Australia

updated 2017 and 2019

The Author is not a lawyer or an accountant and does not intend to render legal, accounting or other professional advice within this book. No guarantees of income, sales or results are promised. It is recommended that users of this book seek legal, accounting and other independent professional business advice before starting any business or acting upon any advice given herein.

ISBN: Paperback 978-0-9871151-0-2
Ebook 978-0-9871151-1-9

CiP data available Australian Libraries.

Also by Ruth Barringham

7 Day Ebook Writing and Publishing System

Goodbye Writer's Block

How To Write An Article In 15 Minutes Or Less

Disclaimer:

The author and publisher have used their best efforts in preparing this Book. The author and publisher make no representation or warranties with respect to the accuracy, applicability, fitness, or completeness of the contents of this Book.

The Author is not a lawyer or an accountant and does not intend to render legal, accounting or other professional advice within this book. No guarantees of income, sales or results are promised. It is recommended that users of this book seek legal, accounting and other independent professional business advice before starting any business or acting upon any advice given herein.

The information contained in this book is strictly for information purposes. Therefore, if you wish to apply ideas contained in this book, you are taking full responsibility for your actions. Whilst we hope you find the contents of this book interesting and informative, the contents are for general information purposes only and do not constitute advice. We believe the contents to be true and accurate as at the date of writing but can give no assurances or warranty regarding the accuracy, currency or applicability of any of the contents in relation to specific situations and particular circumstances.

This Book is not intended to be a source for advice, and thus the reader should not rely on any information provided in this Book as such. Readers should always seek the advice of an appropriately qualified person in the reader's home jurisdiction. The author and publisher of this Book assume no responsibility for information contained in this Book and disclaim all liability in respect of such information. In addition, none of the content of this Book will form any part of any contract or constitute an offer of any kind.

Table of Contents

Chapter 1.

What is the Laptop Lifestyle?

Hello, and welcome to Living the Laptop Lifestyle: How to Start & Grow a Profitable Online Business So You Can Quit Your Job.

My name is Ruth Barringham and I live in Queensland Australia on the beautiful Sunshine Coast. I used to live about an hour south near the city (Brisbane) but once I started visiting the Sunshine Coast and saw how beautiful it was, I knew it was somewhere I wanted to live. And that's the beauty of my Laptop Lifestyle is that I can live anywhere I want.

I've been working online as a writer since the late 1990s/early 2000s.

Before that, I used to work full-time, but once I decided I wanted to be a writer, I moved to part-time work and part-time writing until I was earning enough money to quit my job and work from home as an online writer.

And the freedom this laptop lifestyle gave me enabled me to live wherever I wanted because I can take my business with me anywhere.

And I'm so glad you've also made the decision to move towards your own Laptop Lifestyle (from here referred to as LLS).

Let's start by talking about what an LLS is exactly.

An LLS stems from your laptop computer.

LLS means not having to go out to work anymore. It means no more long commutes to a job you hate, or a job that you have, at the very least, become indifferent to.

It's no fun getting up every single weekday and facing the long drive/commute to somewhere you don't want to be.

To have an LLS all you need is a laptop computer and access to the internet, and with those two things, you can change your life. You don't even have to have access to the internet all the time. I know of some people who work from home as online writers yet they don't even have the internet in their house. Instead, they do their writing at home and then go to a local library or cafe to use the internet.

You need your laptop so you can create a website and build an online business from it, and you need the internet to upload and download files, research, email and a few other things. Though you should be able to do most of your work off-line.

Some people try and run an online business without actually owning a laptop computer. I wouldn't recommend this. If you don't have your own computer you're restricted to when and how long you can work.

Working from internet cafes may sound romantic but these places are busy, noisy and usually quite crowded (not to mention the nosey person sitting next to you, sneaking peeks at your screen to see what you're doing). Also, internet cafes cost money so you have to pay by the half hour or the full hour. They also charge for printing. And logging into your accounts online isn't advisable from a public computer in case cookies remember your details and pass them onto the next person (plus public computers are less secure than private computers).

So it's best to have your own computer and as long as you have access to the internet when you need it, you should be fine. Of course, if you don't have your own computer, then internet cafes (or library computers) will have to do for now.

It's also a common myth that if you use your computer for business, it's better to have a desktop computer. I disagree. A laptop is portable, and these days laptops are as powerful, if not more powerful, than desktop computers.

I have a 13" Mac Book Pro laptop computer. I used to be a dedicated Windows user until my computer hard drive crashed in 2011. I'd always wondered what Mac computers were like because they look stunning in the Apple store in the city.

So I took a closer look at them and bought one. At first it was hard to make the change because Mac computers are so different from Windows computers. But once I got the hang of it I was okay, and, as it turns out, the Mac computer is far easier to use. It's mostly drag & drop which suits me fine. Easy is always my favourite way of doing things.

So from my little Mac Book Pro computer, I run my online business. I also write and publish books and ebooks and I earn all my income from my writing.

Sometimes people ask me how I keep on top of everything. I tell them it's easy because I have so many systems in place so that working is a breeze. I also outsource what I can't or don't like to do and that streamlines how I work even further. Most of the work though, I do myself and after doing it for so many years, I have a good idea of what I'm doing.

And unlike other businesses, you don't need to keep a stockpile of whatever you're selling. In fact, the LLS isn't about buying and selling anything. It's about working whenever and wherever you want with your laptop computer and (sometimes) an internet connection. And I'm going to show you exactly how to do it.

The LLS also means you won't be working for other people. I've seen too many people set up an online business only to have to rely on 'clients' commissioning work from them. And soon the clients get overbearing, demand too much, complain about the work that's done for them, which shatters the dream of living an LLS because it ends up being harder work than going to a job every day.

Nope, the LLS is not about working for someone else. It's about you, your laptop and making money online.

And it gets even better than that.

The LLS is not about making money. It's about making money from something that you love to do or something you love to read/watch/talk about.

In other words, it's about making money from something you're interested in. And when you can make money from it, you wake up excited in the mornings and look forward to the day ahead. And it keeps you up late at night because you want to keep going.

Can you imagine a life like this?

And it doesn't even matter if you don't know what you're going to make your online business about, because within the pages of this book, you're going to discover what it is you love to do AND how you can make money from it.

And it's going to be easy and a lot of fun.

The LLS is also not about full-time work. It's about working part time so you have more time to live your life.

Of course, you may love your new LLS work so much (because it never seems like work) that you want to do it all day. Well, that's fine too if it's what floats your boat.

And it doesn't matter how much or how little you work, because your new LLS will create wealth in your life.

What is wealth?

Most people think only about money when they think of wealth. But the LLS is much more than that.

Wealth is money PLUS time.

Money is no good on its own if you don't have the time to enjoy it.

And time is no good on its own if you don't have money to enjoy it.

I know that there are plenty of people who say that money can't buy happiness... yada, yada, yada. But in this materialist society we live in, you need money to enjoy life more. I'm not talking about untold riches, I just mean enough money to live your life the way you want to, rather than living only the way you can afford. That's why the wealth that your new LLS will bring you is money AND time.

And your new LLS will also make it possible to choose your own working hours.

Some people (like me) are morning people and work far better in the earlier hours of the day. I personally love to get up early, work for 3 or 4 hours and finish at lunch time. Other people like to sleep in and work later in the day. While others like to have the days to themselves and then work in the evenings.

But whichever hours you choose to work, it'll sure beat working 9 to 5 for someone else, which is the way you're probably working at the moment.

Your LLS is also about not doing what you don't want to do. Don't get me wrong, you'll still have to wash your dishes and clean your clothes, but when it comes to earning money, you can choose for yourself what you work on.

But just remember that it will be work. You do actually have to sit down and do something. The only difference will be that you'll enjoy it.

You'll also have the luxury of working from anywhere.

I've been living the LLS for several years now and the place I love to work from the most is home. I know that you may think that working from my own house is not exactly 'escaping', but I love where I live and I like to sit at home and work on my big wooden deck where I can see for miles. I live in a place that's sub-tropical. That means we have mild winters, humid and hot summers, palm trees in the garden and cool breezes to sit and work in.

So why would I want to work anywhere else?

In the future I do have plans to buy a camper van (similar to a Kombi van, but bigger) and travel a lot. Although for now I'm happy at home. But my LLS gives me the freedom to travel when I want to - and I do want to travel and I will.

I also have plans to move to a luxury apartment at the coast, and the freedom of my LLS means I can live anywhere and just take my business with me. And taking my business with me is as easy as picking up my computer, my desk diary and my internet dongle, and taking them wherever I go.

And the LLS gives me time to have a life. I get up in the mornings, check my emails after breakfast, check my diary to see what I'll be working on. I then work a few hours, upload/download a file or two and I'm done for the day. In the afternoons I swim, read, watch a movie, or spend time with my husband, who works at home too, helping me with my publishing company.

Once you build up your own online business, which you're going to do simply and easily, you'll soon realise that how much money you make is entirely up to you.

You might do things that bring in a lot of money and you might do things that don't.

And that's good news because everyone is different and every online business is different and so as you go along you'll soon figure out what works for you, what doesn't work for you, what you want to do more of and what you need to do less of.

And it WILL be fun, as well as profitable. Even if you think you're not earning enough money from what you're doing, you'll find a way to turn it around. We all have to find our own way on the internet, but it's never boring.

As an example (an extreme example) there was a young guy who started working online a few years ago. He set up a website but only managed to earn an average of $1 a day from it. I was watching what he was doing. He wasn't doing much and so wasn't earning much. He didn't have a clue how to make more money from his website.

But he was not deterred at all and decided that if he could only make $1/day from his website, then he would set up 50 websites the same way and earn $50 a day. I thought that was very entrepreneurial of him, in a very low-income kind of way. It made me smile.

So don't worry about earning low amounts of money. That guy was on his own and trying to figure it out himself. You have all the information here to help you every step of the journey.

So don't let anything get in your way.

You're about to embark on the road to freedom from the 9 to 5 grind.

And you can start enjoying it right now.

Chapter 2.

Imaginary Barriers to Starting Your Business

This chapter is called 'Imaginary Barriers to Starting Your Business.' I used the word 'imaginary' because there are no barriers to starting your own online business. There are only false beliefs.

And don't disregard the things I'm going to tell you here, because they really can be barriers that stop you doing what you want to do and I have actually seen these things stop people living their dream.

Believe me, these imaginary things are real dream crushers. That's why I want to take a bit of time to go through them in case there is one that you recognise about yourself, so you know that you're not the only one with that problem and to let you know that you can overcome it.

Don't think that this is all a bit of Pollyanna mumbo-jumbo. It's definitely not. These barriers can seem real and they can stop you if you let them.

But don't you let them:

The Age Barrier

One of the most common barriers people try and use is age. They imagine they are either too young and stupid or far too old to learn anything.

Both of these are a load of rubbish. No one is too young or too old to learn. Why would they be? Young people can learn anything (school proves this) and your brain doesn't stop learning just because you get older.

Age is not a barrier to doing anything.

Lack of Experience

Experience, or lack of it, isn't a barrier at all because you're about to learn everything you need to know. In fact it's probably better if you don't know anything. That way you can start with a clean slate and no bad habits or false beliefs.

Creating websites and making money online isn't hard. It's just different. It's like me with my Mac Book Pro computer. When I first bought it I thought I'd made a terrible mistake. It was nothing like a Windows computer. There wasn't even a right click on the mouse pad! Holy moly! How was I supposed to work when I kept right clicking and nothing was happening? And it wasn't called a mouse pad anymore. It was now a track pad.

Too many differences.

Every time I wanted to delete a file, I was used to right-clicking on it, choosing delete, clicking yes I was sure I wanted to delete it and then it would disappear to the recycle bin.

But now I had no right-click, so I had to Google how to delete files on a mac computer. It seems I had to left-click and hold down the file and drag and drop it into the Trash Can (not called a recycle bin any more) in the bottom corner of the screen. How simple was that? Once I got used to how different the Mac computer was I found it so much easier to use.

And that's what you'll find with creating your own online business. It may all seem completely alien to you right now, but it's really all quite simple. So lacking experience doesn't matter at all.

Fear of Failure

No one wants to be a failure. So why would you tell yourself you will?

The law of attraction is always at work. Think you'll fail, and you're right. Think you'll succeed, and you're right.

And supposing - just supposing - that you did fail to create a successful online business or you didn't start making as much money as you wanted to. You haven't failed. You've learned what not to do.

Or you can create 50 websites and make 50 times the amount of money. ☺

Just don't sit there and say you won't try in case you fail. You won't fail. But you will learn a lot.

Fear of Success

Just as fear of failure can stop people starting something, so can fear of success.

No one really thinks about being afraid of succeeding, but it happens all the time. Success means a change in your life. Change is scary. Therefore you get a fear of succeeding.

I once had a brilliant idea for an online business. I love sewing and I wanted to buy an embroidery machine. I'd been looking at them in the shops and fell in love with them. Then I had a brilliant idea to create a website selling embroidered blouses. I thought about it for weeks and thought of how I could do it, how many blouses I'd need to sell to make a decent living. And it all looked like it could work out really well.

My idea was to sell top-quality hand made blouses that were made out of top quality cotton, sewn with sturdy seams and embroidered all down the button hole band, along the collar and the top of the pockets with beautifully embroidered patterns.

Oh yes, my blouses were going to sell like hot cakes (well, sell like blouses really) because they were going to be so beautiful and so unique. I even had a friend in mind who was an excellent seamstress. She made herself and her daughters beautiful clothes all the time and I figured that if my business got really busy I could call upon her sewing skills to help out.

But then I thought that it wouldn't take much for me to be overwhelmed with work. More than two orders a day and I wouldn't be able to handle it. Then I started to panic that my business would get too much too quickly and become a bigger success than I could handle.

So I didn't do it. I never started my business. And to this day I always wonder, what if...? It never occurred to me at the time that I could stop people from ordering if I got overwhelmed. I just panicked about the success I knew it would be.

Ridicule

This is something that is really hard to bear. Whenever you start a new venture, something that's really different than what you normally do, you'll find that there seems to be a whole line of people queuing up to ridicule you if you fail. I don't think the queue of people ever exists but it certainly feels like it.

And if there is anyone who's waiting for you to fail so that they can smirk and say "I told you so," you'll probably find that it's someone who is less successful than you. It's always the "wanna bees" who are quick to judge.

So if anyone does have a nasty comment to make, just ask yourself whether the person has achieved more than you. And I think you'll find they haven't.

Fear of Loneliness

No one wants to feel lonely and that's sometimes how working from home can be perceived. But the difference is, you won't be lonely. Yes, you'll be alone, but being alone is very different to being lonely.

Lonely is a feeling, not a physical state of being. That's why it's possible to feel lonely in a crowd.

When I'm at home working, I'm either so engrossed with what I'm doing that time flies by and so I don't even think about other people, or I don't feel alone because I'm emailing with someone somewhere in the world, or I'm talking on the telephone with somebody.

Lonely? I'm never that. I know at least 2 people who work online and they start work early in the morning and love what they're doing so much that sometimes it's 10 o'clock at night before they realise it. Now that's the kind of work day that I love to have.

Lack of Organisation

To be successful online you need to be super organised. All your files, virtual and paper, need to be filed somewhere neatly and organised in such a way that everything is easy to find.

On my computer I have a folder called Books. Inside that folder I have a folder for each book I've written. The separate folders are so that if I make notes, I can keep them with the book they belong to. I have another folder called Websites. In that folder I have a separate folder for each website. I also have a folder called Letters, Article Ideas, and so on. Inside each folder everything is filed away into separate folders. You'll also notice that I give my folders simple names so that I don't have to open them to find out what they are. Even if I download something from the internet (an ebook for instance), I change the name straight away to something simple so that I know what it is at first glance.

Keeping my files and folders stored in this way isn't difficult. I just have to spend 2 seconds thinking about where to store a document on my computer. I also have my paper files stored neatly into Lever Arch files by subject and each document is in date order with the newest files at the top so that every new file simply has to go at the front of the file.

When I get mail/email, I deal with it straight away so that it doesn't get backed up. My system for dealing with both snail mail and email when it arrives, is file it, deal with it, pass it on (if it's for my accountant/book keeper or someone else) or bin it. I rarely have more than half a dozen emails in my inbox at any given time. I deal with everything as it comes to me, or if I don't have time to answer an email immediately (or I need to think about it), I move it to the Drafts folder so that I don't forget it. The only thing I ever keep in the drafts folder are emails waiting to be answered so as soon as I see there's something in it, it reminds me to deal with it.

So if you're usually a bit disorganised, just start as you mean to go on. Start your new venture in a simple organised way, and stick to it.

Not Being Good With Financials

One big sticking point in running your own business is dealing with the financial side of things. And by that I mean doing all the paperwork.

I am hopeless when it comes to bookkeeping. At home I'm fine dealing with the household budget (in fact I can be quite fanatical about it sometimes) but when it comes to dealing with tax, form filling and balancing books, I just cringe and turn away.

The easiest thing to do (I find) is to print off all my receipts and invoices and store them in a big metal tin. That way anything I've bought or received money from, I have the paperwork to show it all.

I print off a balance of all my online accounts (more about these later) at the end of every month. That way I know how much I've earned and how much is owing.

It's easy to make up an accounts sheet to write it all on, just to keep things tidy and easy to see at a glance. I give all my information to my book keeper, who also deals with my quarterly tax returns/payments, and at the end of every financial year the whole lot gets shipped off to my accountant, and she, bless her little cotton socks, produces an end of year statement which is several pages long.

When you start off you won't need an accountant, unless you do exceptionally well and make thousands of dollars straight away (and I really hope you do). So for the first year just enjoy the ride of working online and earning money.

If you're at all unsure, you can always Google about tax laws for small businesses where you live or do it when you start making money. You could also contact a book keeper/accountant and ask them what you should do.

For a small business, paying for bookkeeping/accounting shouldn't be very expensive because your accounts will be simple, unlike physical businesses that have to deal with bank loans, premises, staff wages, insurance and so forth. Compared to that, your financial accounts will be a walk in the park for a professional.

But worry about that when it happens. For now just concentrate on getting your business up and running.

No Time

Whenever we have to start incorporating something new into our lives we complain about our lack of time. We talk about how difficult it is to 'find the time' to do things.

But time cannot be found because it's not lost. Time just keeps ticking every second of every day. Everyone in the whole world, rich or poor, has the same amount of time. The only difference is what we do with it.

If you want to have time to do something new, then you have to give up doing something else.

For instance, you could spend less time watching TV, or less time in the bathroom (if you're a bathroom lingerer) or less time gossiping with friends, or less time socialising. And if you usually go out drinking with your friends at night, don't expect them to be supportive when you say you want to leave early to go home and work on your website. They won't understand at all.

Time is always moving on.

The question is, are you?

No Money

This is a favourite. "I can't afford it."

Yes you can. Everyone, and I mean everyone, can find some spare money if they need to.

Compared with off line businesses, starting an online business is cheap. All you really need is a bit of money to register a name for your website and to buy a hosting package so you can get it online. This can be done for around $100/year with most companies.

So where can you find the money?

Cut backs. Whenever I need money for something, I always cut back on something unnecessary. As an example, when we were having renovations done on our house, we spent a year or two saving up for it (it was extremely expensive because we wanted to do it right). So we only had one holiday (we usually have about 3), we stopped eating out, we made cheaper food at home with lots of rice, beans and pasta and filled the freezer with lots of homemade goodies. We also cut back in a few more places like clothes buying, gift buying, etc.

So if you need money for your website start up, stop eating steak and start eating more pasta. I once came across a website online all about cooking cheap food. It was started by someone who said they thought food was expensive till they realised that pasta was only 99 cents a bag. That was enough to set them on a mission to see how cheaply, and healthily they could eat. And it turned out he saved thousands in just one year.

If you need more proof that food is cheap take a look at https://www.livebelowtheline.com.au/. This is a yearly challenge across the UK, US, NZ and Australia for people to live on just $2 a day for food with the money saved and sponsor money going to charity to educate children living in poverty to help lift them out of it. And every year people participate and complete the challenge. They say it's not easy. But it's not impossible.

My point about all this is that money can be saved from one area of your life to be used in another. Even someone on welfare could buy cheaper clothes or ask for cash instead of gifts for birthdays or Christmas.

And after saying all that, it is possible to start an online blog for free with a good service like Google's blogger.com.

So lack of money can't stop you because you can set up an online business for free.

Too Impatient

Beginning your laptop lifestyle has to be started how you mean to go on - gradually. It's not a race, it's not a get rich quick scheme. It's a change of lifestyle that you can begin part time. And because you want your new business to last you need to put some thought into it and not just rush ahead and try and create a business you think you can make tons of money with.

You need to enjoy what you do because it's going to become your life's work. So forget the fast track to riches idea. These things never last, or worse, they don't work at all.

Starting gradually doesn't mean going at a snail's pace. On the contrary, the sooner you start the sooner you make money. But it's not all about money. It's about a better lifestyle. And because it can be done in your spare time, there's no need to rush.

Just begin, and once you get it right, and before you know it, you'll be ready to quit your job.

Fear of Quitting Your Job

At first quitting your job and working for yourself sounds really great. But when it comes to the reality of actually doing it, it can seem scary.

But there's no need to fear. You don't HAVE to quit your job. No one is going to make you stop working if you don't want to. And I'd advise not quitting at all until you're sure you can support yourself from your online income, or before you're comfortable with quitting.

Some people, and I've known a few, spend a year living frugally while they set up their online business and save up 6 month's to a year's worth of income. That way, when they do actually quit their job, they have enough money to live on "just in case."

Having a financial safety net like this is always advisable no matter what the circumstances. I ALWAYS have a financial safety net; an amount of money I can draw on for up to 6 months or more, should my income suddenly cease for any reason.

I hate living pay-day to pay-day and so should you. That is a terrible way to live, knowing that if you missed just one pay-day you'd be in financial trouble.

I much prefer to have a money back up. In fact, I'm pretty sure that if I didn't earn any more money for the rest of the year (and it's only February now), I could cut back on my spending, eat and live frugally, and survive without income until next year.

And that's a wonderful feeling, knowing I have some money behind me that I can draw on and I'm very good at being frugal. It's pretty much the way I live anyway. I'm not a big spender and I absolutely HATE shopping, especially clothes shopping. Which is probably why I don't have many clothes.

And I can cook for my family for a week on practically nothing because I know that pasta, rice and beans are cheap AND healthy, and we have quite a sizeable vegetable garden at home and we also grow a few herbs and have a number of fruit trees too, including peaches, plums, bananas, citrus (lime, lemon, orange, grapefruit and mandarine), mango, mulberries, paw paws (papaya) and more. And we don't even have a big garden. We just pack a lot into it.

Financial back ups are great and so is having food growing at home. I'd recommend both things to everyone right now. If you don't grow food at home, you should because it's not hard. Plants like to grow, in fact they demand it (especially the weeds) and our veggies survive really well, even with a few weeds around them.

And having a financial back up makes so much sense that I'm sure I don't have to tell you why it's a good thing to have.

So don't worry about quitting your job. Although this whole book is about establishing an online business so that you can quit your job and live the laptop lifestyle, you don't have to quit your job if you really don't want to, or you can work part time and run your own online business too. It's your choice and it's entirely up to you. No one can quit your job for you or force you to do it, so don't worry.

But I'm betting that once you start working online you'll love it so much you won't want to work as an employee anymore.

I've been working online now for over 15 years. I started off creating websites in my spare time while I worked full time. I then changed jobs and took on part time work so I could work at home more.

Then eventually I stopped working altogether and just continued working online for myself.

And I've never looked back and I sure as hell haven't missed working as an employee.

Chapter 3.

In The Early Days...

When you first start out establishing your own online business, you'll find it all so alien and you'll be so busy - or so it will seem.

You see, in the beginning, you have a steep learning curve to climb. If you've never built your own website or earned money online, then you will have more to learn then most. And even if you have built your own website before and made some money from it, you're about to learn how to do it for a living, which is different from just making a bit of money.

For years I spent time online making money here and there but never needing it to rely on as my sole income. But once I started taking it seriously, I spent time looking around the internet, seeing what others were doing (or claiming they were doing whether it was true or not) and trying a few things out.

Eventually I realised that I didn't want to try and make lots of money fast. One reason was because I didn't think it was really possible to do it, at least not the way the so-called "gurus" were saying it. It all seemed too much like cheating people just to make some fast money. And schemes like that can't last long.

For instance, one of the highest selling money-making ideas at this time of writing, was called the Mass Income Multiplier and it claimed that without any work on your part, this piece of software (that you could buy for a mere $49) would create for you "awesome auto money pages within 30 seconds."

Imagine that. You don't have to write a thing. You just use this software to create web pages and then you just sit back and make money. Does it sound too good to be true? You bet it does.

There is also the danger online (and I've fallen for this before myself) of seeing that someone is doing the same thing as me online but is doing it slightly differently, so I start to think that I should be doing the same as them because, maybe, just maybe, I'm missing out on something or I'm doing it wrong.

But doing that is not living the laptop lifestyle. It's competing with others online who may be lying about how well they're doing, or what they're doing might not be the right thing for you. This kind of thinking, that you should be doing something the same way that others do, is something that's all too easy to get caught up in. And it's usually not the right way to go.

Of course, if you come across a brilliant idea, go with it. But if it doesn't excite you, leave it alone.

Remember the saying; "different strokes for different folks." One size doesn't fit everyone. You need to do only the things that you enjoy doing and that help you to earn money, and not the things you feel you should be doing, but you really don't want to.

It's far better to stick to the set-for-life plan of a laptop lifestyle. You'll be so glad that you did.

You'll Soon Be Living a Different Life

Changing from a 9 to 5 job to living the laptop lifestyle, is not just a change of style, it's a change of life.

At first working from home will seem foreign to you, so foreign that you may think you can't handle it. It will feel just TOO different.

But it's a good kind of different. It's the type of change of lifestyle that takes away the crazy rushing around and leaves you free to sit at your computer, get your work done and then you're finished for the day.

There is a common belief that because we're given 8 hours a day to do our job, we make it last the full 8 hours. It's believed that it's possible to do the same amount of work in half the time. But because we're paid to work 8 hours, we make our work last that long.

And so it goes when you're working at home. If you sit down and do totally focused work, you can do more in less time.

I read the popular book by Tim Ferris called 'The 4 Hour Work Week.' In it he asks the question, if you could only work for 2 hours a day, what would you do? I loved that question because it made me realise how much work I CAN actually pack into 2 hours especially if it's 2 solid hours of totally focused work without any distractions.

So if you can do it too, you may only need to work 2 hours a day, or as the book title suggests, 4 hours a week. I have to admit that I'm not as focused as I'd like to be.

Even just now, a few paragraphs back, something just reminded me that I needed to order a case of wine. So I stopped what I was doing, went and got my credit card and ordered some wine from Goodwill Wines because the wine I buy from them supports Animals Australia which is a charity that I support in more ways than just money, and also because the wines are vegan. Why did I suddenly decide to buy wine? I'm not sure. Maybe it was something I wrote. But what I should have done was make note to buy wine and then keep writing. See what I mean? I'm not as focused as I should be.

Once you begin your laptop lifestyle, you'll love it once you get used to it and can stay focused to get plenty of work done in the shortest time possible. But, as a side note, if you wanted to stop and buy wine and support a charity at the same time, it's not a bad thing to do.

Don't Expect Too Much Too Soon

When you first begin your laptop lifestyle, or when you begin making money online, don't expect too much too soon. We all do it, but it can be dangerous.

And it's not just money that is the issue here. You can just as easily expect too much work from yourself. I had this problem some years ago. I'd work all day and then feel totally dissatisfied with how little I'd achieved.

Eventually I worked out the problem. I was giving myself too much to do. I was a harsher boss of myself then any boss I'd ever had before.

But because I like my life to be laptop-like and not business-like, I had to learn to slow down.

And you know what? Once I slowed down and stopped stressing about how much I wasn't getting done, I was able to achieve not just more work but BETTER work. Without the added pressure of needing to do more, more, more all the time, I was able to relax and concentrate on what I needed to do in the present moment, and let the rest go.

But it's not just time that can be an issue. You may also think that your income isn't increasing as fast as you'd like it too. The danger is that you might go looking for things to increase your income faster and you might fall for buying things like the Mass Income Multiplier. But don't do it.

Just look at what you're doing, figure out what's working for you and what's not. Then simply cut out what's not working and do more of what is.

Sound easy? It is.

Once you start working on your own online business, you'll soon be able to see what works, what doesn't, what you enjoy doing and what you least enjoy doing. Then it's a matter of adjusting everything. You'll learn more all about this as we go along.

Training Other People

One of the hardest things about having a laptop lifestyle is having other people confuse it with not working. I spent a considerable amount of time training my friends (I don't really have many so it wasn't too hard) to understand that just because I'm at home it doesn't mean I'm not working.

I don't work all day, but when I am working, I like to do it without interruptions. I don't want people calling round for coffee for an hour or two. Not only is it inconvenient and interrupts my flow of work, I don't actually enjoy sitting round, chatting and drinking coffee for an hour or two.

If they were coming to talk to me about their own business or new projects they're working on, then I'd love that. But usually all they want is to talk about their kids or their husbands, blah, blah, blah, and I don't really care about these things. It doesn't help me in any way. It just sucks up my time and then I have less time later for reading or veggie gardening or dog walking. Don't get me wrong, I'm not anti-social. I love to talk to people. But idle chit chat bores me.

So train your friends and family to understand that working time and free time is your time to do as you please, and not to be at their beck and call. It's not easy to do. People, and especially family members, will resist you and try and keep you the same. They don't want you to change because it's not in their best interests.

Resistance is a hard thing to deal with when it's other people who are resisting your change in life.

When I first quit my job to work at home, my family wouldn't even discuss it with me. Even now everyone I know doesn't like to talk about my work. They prefer to pretend I don't work at all.

Mostly I think it's because they don't understand what I do and also because they are a little bit jealous. But their feelings aren't my problem. I love what I do and I plan to do more of it. Just yesterday I bought another website - well, I registered a new domain name and bought a hosting package so I can get it online.

My advice is ignore everyone and get on with what you really want to do.

There is actually a book by that exact name, 'Ignore Everyone', by Hugh McLeod. He started his online business by sitting in bars and drawing little squiggly drawings on cardboard coasters and napkins. He eventually started selling his squiggles online and they became so popular that now people commission him to draw big framed squiggles for thousands of dollars.

How did he do it? He ignored everyone who said he couldn't make a living out of drawing squiggles. The book is a good read and I'd advise buying a copy or borrowing a copy from the library. I love the book and have read it several times. It's very inspiring.

Training Yourself

Other people aren't the only ones who need training to help you settle into your new lifestyle. You need to train yourself as well.

To work efficiently, which is what you want if you don't want to work hard, it's necessary to give yourself a working routine. If you don't have an actual time that you sit down and work every day, you'll never do it. You'll let other things get in the way.

Even the great horror writer Stephen King says that in order to be able to sit down and work every day you not only need a working time, you need a room where you work so that whenever you're in there everyone knows you're working, and so do you.

Some people don't have a working routine, but most do. I work in the mornings because that's when I'm far more creative and far more motivated. Once I come off the computer at lunch time, I get so caught up in other things that the time gets away from me and before I know it the day's over. So if I worked the other way around and did other things first, I'd never get any work done.

But you have to do what's best for you. You might even have to try a few routines out first before you figure out what suits you best. I know some women who fit their work around their kids' school hours. They work early in the morning for a couple of hours before the rest of the family gets up, they work a few hours during the day when the kids are at school, then they work in the evenings once the kids have gone to bed.

So you see it doesn't matter when you work or how you divide it up, you just have to find your own routine and stick to it.

Changes in Priorities

Once you get into the swing of things you'll find that your priorities change. I know that I did.

Before I started working online, I used to always be busy at home taking care of the home and garden. Or I'd be busy at my job thinking that the more hours I worked the more money I could earn and the better off my family would be.

But now my priorities have changed. My online work has become more important to me than any other work I've ever done before. And I love it because I enjoy my work and it's not just my job any more. It's part of my life; a part I chose to have. And I'm enjoying every minute of it.

Your priorities will change too and it will be a change for the better.

You Need The Right Equipment

Too often I come across people who are trying to work online but don't have the equipment they need.

The biggest example of this is the number of people I come across who don't have an adequate computer. Just the other day I received an email from someone complaining that they wanted to buy a PDF ebook of mine but their computer was old (from 2007) and they thought the ebook would be too slow to download.

PDF ebooks are small files. They're just text documents. If a computer can't download a small file, it must be a terrible computer. I cannot understand how anyone can expect to work online without a good computer.

If there is one thing you've just gotta have in this line of work, it's a good computer. You need to have at least 8GB of memory, a really fast processor and really good graphics. Just these things alone are essential and all new computers have them.

I buy a new laptop computer every 4 to 5 years. I don't try and upgrade the one I have because I think that computers are very complicated pieces of machinery so I need the best I can get, and not a patched up old computer.

And because portable hard drives are so cheap now, it's possible to back up your computer completely so that when you buy a new one, you can simply install all your documents and settings onto your new computer so that it will be as though nothing has changed.

I back up my computer every week (or every day if I'm working on a new website or new ebook). My Mac Book Pro does a back up in such a way that when I had to get a new computer, I just plugged in my portable hard drive and it downloaded absolutely everything from my old computer onto my new computer including all my emails, my settings, my desk top wall paper, my documents, my personally installed software, and everything else besides. It was as though I was running my old computer in a new shell. I love the security of knowing my computer is backed up so completely.

Another reason that it's important to have an up to date computer, is that new software and apps won't run on old computers. Microsoft and Apple update their operating systems all the time so you need a new computer so that you can run standard software and other applications.

And I don' think having the best computer is the only 'must have.'

Because I do a lot of writing I always like to have the best hand writing equipment too. I usually work by writing things out by hand at first because it's keeps the creative part of my brain alive more. I then sit and type it all out onto the computer.

So because of this I like to have nice journals and notebooks to write in. I also write with a mechanical pencil because it's easier to write with. I find that I have to grip a ball point pen a bit harder than I do a pencil. It might not seem like such a big difference but when I'm writing thousands of words at a time, it DOES make a big difference. I find that with a mechanical pencil, the words flow effortlessly onto the paper which I prefer to applying pressure (no matter how light) to make the little ball roll across the page with a ball point pen.

I don't like to think too much when I'm working either. I don't want to have to worry about whether or not my computer's good enough for the tasks I want it to do and I don't want my hand to ache when I have a lot of writing to do. I just want to get on and do my work. That's why it's important to have the best equipment to do the job.

Patience, Grasshopper

As I said earlier, I sometimes used to get frustrated with not getting everything done that I wanted to do in a day. And it wasn't until I realised that it wasn't me that was too slow, it was just that I was giving myself too many things to do.

I was rushing too much.

I didn't have patience

I also didn't realise how long it takes to do each task.

I'd put things in my diary like, 'create new website template' and while that might sound like a simple task, it's not a task. It's a whole project.

I should have broken it down into 'create top banner for web page template' and 'find a design for the template' and then 'create new web page template.'

And once it's broken down it's easy to see that it might not be possible to do all those things in one day for a novice like me. I'm not a professional designer so I don't work quickly. I can easily spend a whole day just deciding on the layout for a new template, depending what needs to go on it.

So don't be too harsh on yourself either. Make sure that you allow plenty of time for each task you need to do, or better still, don't give yourself a time limit.

In the end you'll find (as I have done) that the more time you spend on something, the more attention to detail you can give it and the better it turns out.

1,000 Hours and 10,0000 Hours

There's a well known saying that if you want to be good at something you need to do it for 1,000 hours, and to master it, you need to do it for 10,000 hours. And I believe that's not far off the mark.

Breaking down the math of all this, it means that if you want to be good at something you need to do it 8 hours a day for 125 days, and if you were working 5 days a week, the 125 days is 25 weeks, which is half a year.

And if you want to master it, 10,000 hour is 1,250 days if you work 8 hours a day, and if you were working 5 days a week that would be 250 days, 50 weeks a year is 5 years worth of 8 hour days to master something.

Why am I telling you this?

So that in the beginning, you won't feel that you need to do too much or that you need to be perfect. You can be good in 6 months. You can be great in 5 years. And if you're smart and focused on your work, you can dramatically decrease these times.

Whatever Suits You Is Fine

Just do whatever suits you. Don't go thinking that because other people online are doing things differently that you need to copy them. You don't. You're not them and they're not you. They enjoy doing things a certain way and you'll enjoy doing it differently. There's no right or wrong. There's just different.

It can be all too easy to get caught up in all the online hype and think that if you're not doing what the so-called 'gurus' say you should be doing then you'll never make it. You'll never succeed.

Just remember that behind everything uttered online by a 'guru' is a product they're trying to pitch. They're always trying to sell you something. No one works for free. Not even the 'gurus'. In fact, especially not the 'gurus'. They're in the whole online thing to make mega bucks. They don't want satisfactory returns for their time. They want fat returns. That's why they always promote high ticket items and they expect a fast turnaround. That's why their online sales pitches always look so hyped. Most of them are.

If it was possible to do all the things they say it's possible to do like making money just by buying something from them and performing what they usually describe as doing "one click" and making thousands of dollars from it, don't you think we'd all be doing it?

And I can tell you right now, there is nothing you can buy in the whole world that just takes "one click" to make it automatically earn you thousands of dollars.

This doesn't mean that any money you earn will have to be hard earned. On the contrary, the laptop lifestyle is all about not working too hard or having to do things you don't want to do.

You will have to work.

The only difference is that it won’t feel like work.

Chapter 4.

Investing in Your New Business

Money is one of the biggest issues in most people's minds when it comes to setting up a new business venture. It's definitely something I always think about and you probably do too.

And you should be wary. So many times online I see people selling their 'formula' for making thousands of dollars a month online. And they convince buyers by demonstrating how much they made themselves. And I don't doubt that it's true and they did make a lot of money.

But what they don't tell you is that in order to earn all these thousands, you also have to spend quite a bit too so the money they claim they earned isn't all profit. They've probably spent most of it already.

So will you need to invest a lot of money in your new online business?

Well, it's like giving an answer to the question "How long is a piece of string?"

How much money you spend or don't spend is entirely up to you. And even if you don't have any money to spare right now, that's okay too because I'm going to tell you how you can set it all up for free. Of course buying what you need is far better in the long run than using what's free online. But it's entirely up to you.

You can register a domain name and buy a year's hosting package to get your website online for around $100 a year. These are the two basic necessities you're going to need, as you'll soon learn. You can, of course, use a free blogging service instead, but it won't be as flexible as having your own site.

These types of free blogging services have restrictions on what you can and can't put on your website/blog. They also sometimes put ads on that you don't want, but you don't get any choice. On the other hand there are quite a number of people who have a free online blog and do really well. But it comes back to what I said before; different strokes for different folks. We'll go into it all in great detail soon.

But any business needs a certain amount of financial investment and as you go along you'll come across things you need to buy to make your online work easier. As an example, at the moment I'm considering buying Dragon Naturally Speaking Software. It's not cheap but I've heard so many people say they use it and that it makes writing ebooks so much faster.

So I'm currently sitting on the fence and wondering whether I need to buy it. It does come with a set of headphones/microphone and is said to be 99% accurate in understanding speech, but the question is would the investment of around $200 be worth it. Would it increase my income by helping me to work faster?

Because I can already type fast, at up to 100wpm, I'm not sure that speech to text software would make me any faster. I currently use Pages for Mac word processing software which was free with my computer. I like it because it has a full-screen mode where it makes the page I'm working on float to the front of the screen and it blacks out the background to make writing more distraction free.

Over the years I've bought plenty of products and paid money to have other people do work for me (stuff I can't do or don't want to do) and all of it has made my working life easier and more profitable.

But at the beginning I never would have known I needed all these things. I just learnt as I went along and somehow, probably because I took my time and wasn't hasty, everything turned out just perfectly.

Another investment you'll need to make is time. In fact, it will be your biggest investment. And it would be fair to say that it's not only your time that you'll be investing, but also your attention.

Time is what makes an online business work. Not just the time you put into it, but also, the time it takes for your income to grow. I find that the longer I have a website, the more popular and profitable it becomes. I suppose that's because it takes a while for everyone all over the world to discover it. A global audience is one that takes time to find you online, unless you do something really stupid in public, and someone videos it and puts it on YouTube THEN you go viral in minutes, but for all the wrong reasons. ☺

So over time, while people are still discovering your website, you can use the time to make sure that what they discover will be worth the wait.

Of course there are things you can do to make sure people discover your website sooner, and we'll be looking at this in chapter 11.

In the beginning, though, you'll find that your income is quite sporadic. It can be feast one day and famine the next. But that's how it always is online most of the time, although sometimes it can be feast for several weeks/months at a time, which is my favourite time of all.

What you need to do is look at what your average income is so you can have a better idea of how much you're earning. And during the times of famine, look at what you're doing, or more precisely what you're not doing, and make changes. Doing more is never a bad thing, but doing less is a no-no (unless you're away on holiday). Also things can be seasonal so take note of the times of year that your income is lower to see what you can change. For instance, if it's around Xmas, could you be doing a Xmas sale, or using more seasonal content?

But again, time is a wonderful thing with an online business, because as it goes by, your income will increase and probably become more settled.

IF YOUR NOT GROWING YOU'RE DYING

Working online is a time of growth. There is always something new to learn. That's not to say that you should jump on every band wagon that comes along. But you should at least take a look at things and see if they're for you.

Sometimes you'll find that even though everyone else is doing something and doing quite well at it, it's not for you. For example, everyone now is on Twitter or Facebook.

A lot of people (my friends, family and other online entrepreneurs) tell me that a Facebook account is a must-have and that I can make much more money if I have a Facebook page and lots of 'likes.' But Facebook bores me. I'm not a forum/Facebook/Twitter/social networking person at all. And when I look at the people who tell me that I SHOULD have a FaceBook account, they are either not people who make money from it themselves, or they have another agenda, like trying to sell me their latest ebook about how to make money using social media.

I do have a Twitter and a Facebook account now (although I was slow to do it) but I don't use them much and I prefer to let social media help people find me and my websites rather than use my websites to help people find me on social media. I just don't see the sense in that.

When I opened a Google+ account (which is now, as of 2019, a defunct service), it was only because I thought Google was THE search engine and it wouldn't be long before they started indexing all their own Google+ pages. And I was right. So now I have my blog posts set to be automatically posted on my Twitter and Google+ accounts and so they show up in Google search results.

But I don't worry about it any more than that, because social networking, as it's called, is not something I'm into. It really doesn't float my boat which is probably why I'm not very good at it. But it does get a lot of people to my sites, even though I only use it to automatically post my blog posts.

But all that aside, working online is a life of perpetual growth and learning. I find that no matter how many books and other products I buy, there is always something else I don't know. So I'm always learning. And it seems I'm not the only one. When I talk to others who are working online, they are doing the same as well. They're all buying new things and reading and learning all the time.

And I love it. I love to be learning all the time. They say that you're either growing or your dying and I believe that's true. Working online means you need to be moving forward every day. I'm sure that rarely a day goes by when I don't learn something. Sometimes it can be something simple that I read in an email or something that I see on someone's website. And it gives me a little "a-ha!" moment.

I once read an article (well, more like a short paragraph) online called "No More Yes. It's Hell Yeah or No." It was all about how you can judge whether something is what you want by your immediate reaction to it, and that if it doesn't make you go "hell yeah!" then the answer should be no. I thought it was a really good idea so I started applying it to my own life and it really simplified things.

If I was in a shop and was in a quandary as to whether to buy something or not, I'd apply the "hell yeah!" technique and if it didn't make me want to say "Hell Yeah!", I'd walk away. Or if someone invited me somewhere and I didn't know if I wanted to go I'd use the technique again. It made everything so much simpler than trying to make up my own mind. And since that day my life has been "Hell Yeah!" or "No!".

You can read the original article at http://sivers.org/hellyeah.

This simple technique has freed up so much time for me and also helped in my online buying decisions. Over the years I've probably bought hundreds of products, books and ebooks. Thankfully there have been very few that I wasn't satisfied with, but that wasn't the fault of the hell yeah technique. That was false advertising, but on each occasion I requested and received a refund.

When I wanted to make money as a freelance writer, I bought a copy of the Quick Cash Writing course. When I wanted to write my first book I bought Write Any Book in 28 Days or Less. When I wanted to learn how to build web pages I took a course in web page design (that's not available any more). When I wanted to create and update websites faster I invested in Adobe Dreamweaver software (which is currently only available as a monthly subscription). And on it goes.

One of my investments was an ebook about writing ebooks that attract more customers, or as the title calls them "Desperate Buyers." It's an amazing ebook, hundreds of pages long and I've already used it to generate dozens of future ebook ideas.

But my purchases have all been sensible and each one gave me a "hell yeah" feeling as soon as I read the sales page.

Please don't ever confuse "hell yeah" with hype. Some sales pages are so full of hype and their claims are so outrageous it's unbelievable. But these writers are so good at what they do that you may feel compelled to buy, buy, buy. But don't, don't, don't.

Some of these sales pages are so convincing that they give you a false "hell yeah" feeling. It's probably because they seem to know where your hot buttons are and how to push them. Some, however, don't have a clue, but they try anyway.

Now enough of telling you what's wrong and what's right.

It's time to get down to work and begin creating your new laptop lifestyle.

Chapter 5.

Generating A Great Business Idea

In this chapter you are actually going to get down to work and decide what your new online business is going to be all about. Don't skip this chapter. Even if you think you know what you want to do, read through all the information here because you might find something else that gives you a "Hell Yeah!' reaction. It might be something you never even considered before, or maybe you did consider it but couldn't see how you could build a business from it.

I used to be the same way. I have lots of things I like to talk about and things I like to do but I couldn't see a way of making any money out of them.

But it seems that you can make money online from just about anything. I say 'just about' because there might be something that you can't make money from, but if there is, I haven't come across it. And please don't try and create an online business around something illegal or offensive.

As long as you have something that you like to do, or a subject that you know a lot about or even just something that interests you, you can build an online business around it.

All you have to do to begin, is to build a website about it.

For instance, I was once pondering this exact fact about is it possible to make money from anything online, even if it's just a hobby?

So I thought about things I like to do and whether I could build a profitable business from them, and I tried to think about the least interesting thing I like to do, and by least interesting I mean it wouldn't be very interesting to talk about it to many other people.

And I thought about knitting. I've been a knitter for most of my life. I still own my first pair of plastic pink knitting needles from when I was 7 years old and my Dad first taught me to knit and I set about knitting the shortest (I only had one ball of wool) and holiest (I kept dropping stitches) scarf the world has ever seen. But boy was I proud of it.

So would it be possible to make money online from knitting?

I Googled knitting and found that there were thousands of different websites all devoted to the subject. Some were information sites selling knitting books and patterns, and some were information sites with instructions for beginners. There were websites selling knitting supplies from balls of wool to huge knitting machines, and others were websites where people were selling handmade items they'd knitted. I even found a website where you can commission someone to knit items for you.

It seems that the craft of knitting is flourishing online and doing very well. There are even websites devoted to selling knitted items from people from all over the world, a kind of eBay for knitters. I had no idea that knitting was so popular. I thought it was all about me, sitting at home watching movies and doing my knitting. But apparently it's not. It's a whole online world of buying selling and making money.

So if I wanted to make a website all about knitting, I could sell what I knit, sell just one certain kind of knitted product (jumpers, toys, tea cosies, wash cloths, etc), sell knitting related products, sell advertising space for other knitters/knitting companies, sell my services as a professional knitter, write about knitting, sell knitting patterns or just blog about my knitting. I could also do all these things.

There may be other ways to make money from knitting but I don't know of any offhand. But even with just what I already discovered, it seems there are many ways to make money from a knitting website. In fact looking at the list above, it looks as if a knitting website could be huge. It could end up as hundreds of pages.

And don't worry about how you'd sell knitting related products or sell advertising. It can all be done automatically without you having to store or ship anything. We'll discuss that later too.

All you have to do right now is think about what it is that you'd like to set up a website about. You don't have to think of how you're going to make money. You just have to choose your subject (niche). And your niche can be narrow. It doesn't have to be broad.

For example. You could set up a website about birds or you could narrow it to wild birds, or pet birds or parrots or even just budgerigars. The beauty of working online means your niche can be as broad or as narrow as you want.

You also need to think about what you want to say about your chosen subject. For instance, say you want to set up a website based on your religion.

Are you going to be talking about religion in general?

A belief in God?

Are you going to try and recruit more members?

Are you going to narrow it down to just the church where you pray?

Are you going to talk about how it affects your life?

Or are you going to sell religious products?

As another example, I have a website about writing at http://ruthiswriting.com. At first it was a website where I sold my services as a freelance writer. But I no longer do much freelance writing so I changed it to a website devoted to teaching others how to become successful online writers. So although the niche of this website stayed the same, the information it contained changed completely.

Before that I used to have a different website for writers, but a few years later, someone contacted me out of the blue and wanted to buy it. At first I said no but they kept upping their offer until I couldn't resist. I also knew that my writing site was only successful because of all the information I had put on it, so all I had to do was set up another writing site and put more information on that and continue earning money from it the same way I did before. Which is exactly what I did. I also couldn't figure out how the other person was going to make money out of my old writing site because it was all about, and written by, me. And to date, the site is just sitting vacant and abandoned and the buyer hasn't made any money from it. Maybe he should buy and read this book. ☺

Right now you may have no idea whatsoever what to make your website about so the following, are some ideas you can use to brainstorm what you want to do.

Business Ideas To Get You Started

Hobbies

This is a simple one as explained earlier. You can make a website all about your hobby or use your website to sell what you create, if your hobby is about making things.

But if you do want to sell what you make then your business won't give you a true LLS because you'll have to store and ship products. A true LLS is about making money only from your laptop computer and an internet connection so that you can work from anywhere.

Topics

This can be any topic that you're interested in. The chances are that if you're interested in something, other people will be too. You need to decide what your website will consist of. Just think that if you could find the ideal website about your favourite topic, what kind of information would it contain?

Life Experiences

If you've been through a traumatic or extremely happy event in your life, you won't be the only one. And there'll be others searching online to find out what happened and how you dealt with it. This is an easy subject to write about because if you've already lived it, you know all about it.

Career Advice

Whatever industry you've worked in, you have knowledge about it. Of course if you had/have a high-flying career then there's a lot you can say about it. But even if you work in retail you can still have a site based on this too. You could talk about job interviews, resume writing, department stores v small shops, customer service, advertising, marketing, wages, promotions, shop lifting...the list goes on. If you've ever had a job, any job, you have information that people want.

Gardening

Something as simple as gardening can be a website paradise. That's because plenty of people have gardens, but not many know what to do with them. Or you could even talk about specialist gardening or exotic plants or growing veggies or growing fruit trees or different types of grass or... Pardon the upcoming pun, but gardening is an evergreen topic.

Buddhism

This is a subject that covers all kinds of areas including buddhist stories (the Buddha used parables to teach and so there is a multitude of teaching stories available), clothing, jewellery, mantras, temples, meditation, different types of Buddhism and living a stress-free, zen-type life.

Book Reviews

If you love reading then a book review website would be right up your street. How great would it be to read books every day and make money?

Amazon is filled with book reviews so even if you don't know how to write a review there's plenty of ideas on the Amazon website. And if you want to work on the go, you could listen to audio books and review them too.

Cooking

Everyone can either cook or wants to cook. And the vast variety of cooking sites you could have are too many to list here. I know if I was going to have a cooking site, it would be a vegan cooking site, because I'm vegan. And if you don't cook, you can still have a website about food.

Collecting

There are millions of avid collectors all over the world collecting all manner of things. Some of these collectors border on being hoarders. If you collect something, antiques, comic books, toys, etc, then you have a niche for a website.

Running

There are so many people in the world taking up running. This topic, along with any other type of health and fitness topic, is extremely popular. You've just got to remember though that because it's popular, there are already millions of websites devoted to this topic so you'd have a lot of competition. On the plus side, it's a very popular topic.

Parenting

If you're a parent, or you've been a parent, you'll know what a maze it is trying to bring up kids and find the right advice. Parenting websites are always popular and the array of items you could be selling to parents for their children is huge. You'll never run out of products to promote, or things to say, if you have a parenting website.

Illness

If you've ever suffered an illness so have millions of others. Illness is a terrible trauma to go through, especially if it's long lasting. So if you've been ill for a long time, you can help others by talking about it online. On the other hand, you could have a website about childhood illnesses which are usually short lived but parents are always looking for information about them.

Health

Health issues are a massive self help topic at the moment, and have been for years. Everyone suffers with their health at some time or other, and those who are healthy are looking for ways to stay that way. Anything to do with health is a winner whether it's diet, fitness, longevity, wrinkles, cellulite, stress management, meditation, natural cures...the list goes on...and on.

Chocolate

There are websites out there devoted to a subject as simple as chocolate. Just Google the word chocolate and it brings up over 800 million results.

Yep, something as simple as chocolate can be big business, especially around Easter time, Valentines' Day and Christmas.

Vegetarianism

The world is thankfully becoming more vegetarian every day. It's partly to do with concerns for animal welfare and partly due to the healthy eating revolution. Either way, it's an extremely popular topic and growing in popularity all the time. You could also look at other types of diet such as vegan, gluten free or macrobiotic.

How to Make Wind Chimes/Dreamcatchers

This is a tight niche but an incredibly popular one. I Googled 'How to make a wind chime' and it came back with nearly 2 million results. When I changed it to 'dreamcatcher' it came back with over 5 million results. So a niche so unusual (or as it seems, not so unusual) as this is very popular.

Art

Whether you're an artist, you have an interest in art or you'd like to sell art, a website devoted to art will be in high demand. It will, however, mean uploading a lot of images. But that's easy to do.

Where You Live

This will be an extremely tight niche, depending on where you live. But local people are always looking for something to do, somewhere to go or want to shop for a bargain. A local website could also appeal to tourists or out of town visitors such as business people. It could also be about the local people.

Kitchens

Anyone who's into interior design will love a website about kitchens. And it doesn't just have to be kitchens. Every room in the house could be a possible website (or web page). You could have a website about designing kitchens, discussing kitchens, selling kitchens, restaurant kitchens, or even kitchen accessories. If you love kitchens, then there will be others who do too or students looking for project information.

Hair Styles

The dead follicles upon our heads, which we commonly call hair, have a whole billion dollar industry built around them. Hair styles are big business and products that keep these styles in place are purchased by the million every day.

Pets

The furry, feathered and scaly creatures who share our homes are another billion dollar industry. These days you can buy more for your pets than ever before. There is now even pet apparel for sale (although I am very much opposed to this stupidity) and dog handbags. These are bags to carry your dog in and not a fashion accessory for your dog. I'm opposed to these bags as well. Dogs aren't ornaments and they love to walk. Pets are big business.

Coping With Loss

Although grief is a terrible thing, it is a sought after subject on the internet. If you've suffered a loss in your life, sharing it can help you and others too. And I know it sounds terrible, but you can also earn money from it. But then again, undertakers have been making money from grieving families for years, so it's nothing new.

Witchcraft

Witchcraft is an accepted way of life now, probably because there's no such thing as a witch that can perform magic. There are white witches as well as dark witches. And witchcraft sites abound all over the internet. A quick search yielded over 28 million results.

Healing herbs

Natural medicine is more in vogue now than ever before. For years herbs were used as medicines before commercial medicines were available. And now more and more people are turning to natural remedies again. So if you know a lot about herbs, or you have an interest in what they can do, you could learn all about them as you build your website.

Garden Birds

Bird lovers never tire of watching birds. And even ordinary people with a garden like to know what types of birds they have and what attracts them. There are millions of books and websites already devoted to this subject so finding information shouldn't be a problem.

World War II

They say that everyone likes to talk about the war. In schools they teach about the war, on the TV we watch movies about the war and on remembrance day we stop for a minute because of the war. The war is certainly a popular topic.

Astronomy

The subject of star gazing and astronomy never goes out of fashion. We have always had a fascination for the stars and what they can predict for us.

Saving Money

The subject of saving money is always of interest to a lot of people. We all like to save money, or to think that we're good at saving money. We like to buy things that will save us money and we like to get a bargain so we feel like we've saved money rather than spent it. And yes, there is a plethora of websites devoted to this subject.

Divorce

This could come under the previous heading of life experiences. But divorce somehow needs a category of its own because it's so huge. No one thinks they will get divorced and it's very complicated and emotional when it happens. And it happens all the time.

Raising Teens

Teens create problems all of their own and that's why they need their own category too. If you've ever tried to raise a teen you'll know how hard it is. They're too big to smack and too young and vulnerable to leave to their own devices. Teens are a problem that parents look online for, for answers.

Short Stories

Websites aren't all about non fiction subjects. Everyone enjoys a short story. Magazines know this and always feature short stories. Some magazines are short story magazines. If your stories are good, people will come back again and again to read more. You can also sell short stories on Amazon as Kindle Singles.

Horror Movies

Horror movies have always held a morbid fascination for many. If you watch horror movies you can build a website around your viewing habits. Old movies, new movies, upcoming movies, memorabilia, actors, movie sets, movie scripts; whatever it is, horror fans like to know.

Star Trek

You wouldn't think that an old TV show like this would have much of a following. Yet when I Googled Star Trek it brought back over 150 million results. And it doesn't have to be just this show. If there's another old TV show that you love, there could be money to be made from it.

TV Comedies

Comedies have to be the most repeated shows on TV. It's now years since the show Friends was last made and yet it's repeated on TV every week day and more than once a day. The Big Bang Theory also seems to be constantly on the TV as well. It seems that every time I turn on the TV there's an episode or two or three on. I don't watch much TV but I bet I've seen every episode of TBBT more than once. So you can take your pick if you're a comedy lover. You can have a website about just one TV comedy or all of them.

I hope the above list has given you some food for thought.

In the coming chapters I'm going to show you how you can make money out of any website, no matter what the niche.

Even if your website is just a small information site, you can make money from it, and I'll show you exactly how to do it.

What you need to do now though, is sit down with a pad and pen and map out what your website will be about and what information it will contain. For instance, if you're planning on creating a website about travel, will it be a site about travel in general, or about places you've visited, or about places to visit where you live or will it be about traveling in the country where you live?

Each of these types of websites will all have completely different information. So if your site was going to be about traveling and holidaying in the country where you live, you might have a page about visas for overseas travellers, you might also have a page for each different city/area and pages stemming from each of these about local places to visit, places to eat, churches, shopping centres, transport and more.

The best way to map out a website (which is the way I do it) is to get a big sheet of paper, draw a square in the middle and call it the home page and from there show links to other pages and from the other pages show the links to even more pages and more pages, etc. Showing a web of pages in this way makes it really easy to see how your website is going to be navigated.

You can also draw how you want your pages to look which also helps you to see what you're creating.

Chapter 6.

Keeping it Simple

I wanted to use this chapter to remind you exactly what the laptop lifestyle is all about.

In the previous chapter we've just been looking at some of the different subjects you can choose to create your website about and how you can make money from them.

But I don't want you to forget that the laptop lifestyle isn't just about making lots of money (although that's always nice). It's all about taking things steady and having a slow and easy life.

This LLS is not an entrepreneur race to the top.

It's about taking one idea at a time that you're passionate about, and working on it to create a profitable online business.

But you need to focus on the passion and not the profit. If you start chasing the money it WILL lead you astray and you WILL get lost. So the focal point of what you're doing is your website, and not how you're going to make money. You will make money, but only if you keep your eyes focused in front of you and look where you're going, not how it's going to profit you.

And your website doesn't have to be big and flashy. On the internet, content is king, not flashy websites. If you want proof of this I can show you two websites that do really well and have tens of thousands of email subscribers and yet the sites themselves are nothing impressive at all. They're just plain.

Take a look at zenhabits.net and theminimalists.com. These guys are just like their websites; plain, honest and hard working. And they built up their online businesses quite quickly without even trying. In fact the Zen Habits website is so plain it's just black text on a white background and nothing else. Not even a heading.

So don't concentrate too much on how your website will look. Just brainstorm for ideas, not ways of making money. If your website has good information people will want to visit. And the more visitors your website gets, the more income you can earn, even if they don't buy anything.

People don't like visiting websites that have no useful information. If they visit once they won't come back. Nor will they tell anyone else about your site.

So don't get caught up in anything you read online about how much money someone else is earning or how much you can be earning.

You need to start by learning the basics and from there you can do anything.

So let's get started by showing you how you can set up and run your own website, even if you've never done it before and you don't know where to start.

You start right here by turning to the next page.

Chapter 7.

Website Creation

This is where it all starts. This is where you have to stop reading and start working on your laptop computer.

Now if you're just reading through this book and decide to come back later and start work on it, what you may read here may sound too technical, but it's not. Once you start working and start building your own website, it will all become clear as you go along.

Building websites isn't difficult. It may all look like gobbledygook if you've never done it before, but once you begin to understand it, you'll realise how simple it is. It's like how I explained earlier about how my new Mac Book Pro computer was so different from my old Windows computer that I didn't have a clue how to use it. But once I figured it out I realised that the Mac computer is actually easier to use than a Windows computer. It just looked harder when I didn't know what I was doing. Now I find it so easy to use I wish I'd bought one years ago.

Website or Blog?

Before you can build a website you need to decide wether you want an ordinary website or a blog.

The difference is only in how you use it. Both work on the same principle.

Websites are created using HTML code which stands for Hyper Text Markup Language. This is simply a set of instructions in computer speak as to how a browser should display a webpage. It tells the browser what colour things should be, where an image should be on a page, where the text should be in relation to the images and how big or small everything should be.

This is how simple html code is:

A web page always begins with <html>. The tags around the letters let the browser know that what's inside is an instruction and not text to display on the page.

This <html> tag tells the browser that it is the beginning of a web (html) page. At the end of the page is </html>. The forward slash always represents the end of something, so in this instance it's telling the browser that it's the end of the web page.

And the forward slash works with every instruction to end it. For instance, the title of a web page that always shows up in the tab at the top of the browser window is put in title tags like this: <title>This is the web page title</title> . These instructions tell the browser where the title begins and where it ends.

Likewise the body of the web page (the part that you see on the screen) is always enclosed by body tags like this: <body>. This is the web page content</body>. And everything has to be put in order so if you were going to create a basic web page the code would look like this:

<html>

<header>

<title>This is the web page title</title>

</header>

<body>

This is the web page content.

</body>

</html>

See how that works? The first tag shows that the web page was starting. Next comes the header tag so that the browser knows that the title is not part of the webpage text. Then the next tag instructs what the text for the title tab will be. The body tag shows what will be on the web page and the final tag has the slash before the html to show that the web page has finished.

Of course web pages get more complicated than that. For instance, if you wanted to centre the words on the page you'd do it like this:

<body>

<center>This is the web page content</center>

</body>

(note the American spelling of the word 'center' which is the only way browsers understand it).

You can also do more, like changing the background colour of the page which would be

<body bgcolor="#ae23db">This is the web page content</body>

Note that you don't need to include the background colour in the end tag. Once the body is finished so is everything that went with it. And colours always start with a hash tag follow by 6 numbers and/or letters.

Naturally there's more to it than that but you get the general idea. It's not difficult. It just takes learning.

So how do you learn how to make a web page?

It's too vast a thing to show you in this ebook, but there are places you can learn it, for free or at a price.

Websites that are good for teaching HTML code (IMO) are http://htmldog.com/ or http://www.w3schools.com/. Both have html tutorials that you can work through.

Another way to learn how to write html code, is to borrow a book from the library or buy a book. The best one to learn from is The Complete Idiot's Guide to Creating a Web Page & Blog. Years ago I bought The Complete Idiot's Guide to Creating a Web Page, because blogs weren't around then and it was a really easy book to learn from.

A blog is slightly different to a website because it's usually written up a bit more informally. Blogs tend, on the whole, to be more personal than business-like. But having said that, there are people out there who use blogs as their only type of online income so blog or website is a personal choice.

With a website you can design the pages yourself and upload them yourself. With a blog you have to log in to an online dashboard and you're limited as to how your blog will look, unless you're a genius at altering blog pages. But you can buy templates for a blog so that the page layout is ready-made.

And unlike an html website, blogs don't have static pages. They are based on html, so you need a knowledge of html code if you want to change your blog in any way, but the pages behave differently because they are dynamic .php files.

PHP stands for Hypertext PreProcessor and the php code is embedded into html files. In a nut shell, what php does is simply instruct the browsers where to place everything before a web page opens. That's why it's called a 'pre' processor. With php the web pages don't actually exist.

The script simply tells the browser how to construct the page before it opens. This is very different from html where all the instructions about layout are embedded into the pages. Php web pages don't contain any data.

Learning php scripting language is not easy and unless you're a scripting wizard I wouldn't even bother going there. You can read more about it and see some tutorials at http://www.php.net/.

HTML is very basic and all websites need it in order to function. And as I said before, even if you decide to set up your website as a blog, you'll need to understand the basics of html code in order to be able to change your blog from the basic template.

So to begin with, go and learn the basics of writing html code and that will give you a really firm foundation on which to build your website.

Learning how to write html code isn't difficult and it shouldn't take long. If you have all the time in the world, you can master the basics in just one week. On the other hand if you only have a couple of hours a day to spare, then it may take you up to a month to learn. But either way it's not hard and you can learn it fast.

While you're learning, you can also begin building your own website (that's what I did) so that by the time you've finished, your website is ready to be uploaded to the internet.

So what I want you to do right now, is buy/borrow a book or visit one of the websites suggested previously, and learn how to build web pages by writing html code.

And as you're learning, use your new knowledge as you go along to build your own website that's ready to be uploaded to the internet.

If you want to have your own blog, you still need to have a good understanding of basic html AND you also need to have the content ready that you'll be putting on your blog.

Later I'll also tell you how you can set up a blog for free.

Getting Web Hosting and a Domain Name

Once you've built your website or have your blog idea in mind the next thing to do is get it all online.

First of all you need a name for your site. It doesn't matter whether it's a blog or a website, it needs a name. And it has to be a name that's not already taken.

To search to see if a name is taken go to a hosting company website. Just go to the hosting company's website, click on 'Domains,' and start searching using the box at the top of the page which will tell you whether or not a domain name has been taken and it will offer alternatives if it has.

But be careful about spelling. I once read a story about a website owner who wanted to call his website Pen Island, and sure enough that domain name was available so he registered it. Sadly, domain names don't have spaces and everyone started reading penisland.net as penis land. That website is still on the internet but whether or not they sell many pens I have no idea.

So before you dive in and register your domain name, check to see how the words run together without a space, and if it looks bad, consider changing it, or hyphenating it.

Hosting companies make it easy for you to register a domain name. Once you've chosen a domain name that's not taken you can register it immediately right on the spot. You can also choose a hosting package at the same time.

A hosting package gives you access to your website control panel where you can upload files, create email addresses for your website, check your stats to see how many people have been visiting your website, and a whole lot more. It also gives you the space on the internet where your website can be found.

In your control panel there is a link to the 'file manager.' This is what you use to upload your files. They should usually be uploaded to your 'public' folder. This is where all your accessible webpages can be seen by the public.

Control panels are easy to use and every available option within your control panel will have a help file to tell you what it does and how to use it. Alternatively, if you have any problems, you can telephone your hosting company.

I like using companies that have 24/7 customer service so that I can call them whenever I want to because being in Australia means I'm in a different time zone to a hosting company that is in the UK or the US. Hosting companies are usually quite patient with beginners, so in the beginning I found that even if I was calling because there's something that I didn't know anything about, they explained it all to me. These days though, I'm pretty savvy with website control panels so I don't need much help.

When I first started out, I used to call them to set up websites. I'd just tell them over the phone what I wanted to call my site and they'd register it for me and set up the hosting package.

One day when I set up a new site, I did it online from their website and within 10 minutes I received an email saying the domain name was registered and the control panel was set up. How fast was that? These guys know that time is money and they don' t keep me hanging around.

Just as an aside...

I don't like to say terrible things about hosting companies, but my first one was Dataflame and it's only fair that I let you know what happened with them.

At first they seemed fine but over the years they went downhill in my opinion. Their 24/7 customer service turned into nothing more than online chat with the person at Dataflame telling me to come back when their offices were open. But they are in the UK (although they try and pretend that they have a US division, but they don't) and I'm in Australia, so I needed them to be available to help 24/7.

Not only that but their down time kept increasing and I was constantly finding my sites to be off-line, and their 24/7 customer service couldn't help me as usual.

I was losing money with my sites being off-line so much and I was totally frustrated with the poor service. So eventually I tried other hosting companies and moved all my websites away from Dataflame, to a couple of different companies.

When I searched online I found a lot of recent complaints about Dataflame so I wasn't the only one thinking their service was poor.

I'm in business online. I need my websites to be online all the time. Dataflame didn't seem to understand that, so it's their loss. And the only reason I'm mentioning them here is to warn you in case you were thinking of signing up with them. I wouldn't personally recommend them to anyone.

Once you have registered your domain name and you have your hosting package, your hosting company will email you details of how to log into your control panel and provide a username and password.

Uploading files through your file manager can be time consuming although it's a very stable way to upload files.

Alternatively you can use FTP to upload files. FTP stands for File Transfer Protocol and is just a simpler way of uploading files.

There are several different free tools you can use to upload files. The first one is called FileZilla. This is a popular piece of software with millions of people using it. Another one (one which I've used) is Cyberduck. Both are available for Mac and Windows computers.

If you want to set up a blog, once you have your hosting package, go into your control panel and look for a link to 'Other Services' or "Software Packages" or something similar. Click on it and this will show you a list of programs you can install on your website including forums, online stores and different types of blogs.

If you're new to all this then it's best to choose a WordPress blog because it's the easiest to install, has a whole ton of online help and millions of 'themes' to choose from, and most of them are free.

Themes are an add-on for a blog that changes its appearance and how it's set out. All you have to do is upload the theme of your choice to your blog, click 'activate' and it installs itself automatically. Wordpress software also comes with a few available themes built in so you just choose how you want your blog to look and click to use the theme of your choice.

With your control panel (known as a Cpanel) all you have to do is click on the type of blog you want to install, choose a user name and password, and your blog will be installed automatically. Then all you have to do is log into you dashboard (bookmark your log-in page so you can find it again easily) and start adding posts, categories, archives and whatever else you want.

Blogs are simple to install, but if you don't have any basic html knowledge, you won't have a clue how to change your blog and personalise it, although you can pay someone else to do it for you if you can explain to them exactly what you want.

An easy way to jump straight into a blog is to use Google's free blogger.com service.

I have one of these blogs at http://writeaholic-inspiration.blogspot.com. As you can see using this service gives you a blogspot.com address online.

These blogs are free to set up. You then login to your blog's dashboard and make changes to how you want your blog to look.

If it all seems daunting, go onto YouTube and do a search for how to use the blogger dashboard. Many people have put up videos about this and they show you exactly how to use them.

Just go to YouTube.com and search for "how to set up a blogger blog" or "how to use the blogger dashboard" or something similar. There is a really short-yet -helpful video on youtube that shows you how simple Blogger is to use at http://www.youtube.com/watch?v=rA4s3wN_vK8. Just take a look and you'll see what I mean. If you feel at all overwhelmed with how to set up a blog, this short video will rest all your fears because blogger is so simple.

Also, once you login to your Blogger blog, you'll see that in the menu there is a help link. If you click on it, it will open a page that lists everything you need to know about how to set it up to how you want it and how to use the blog.

On your blog you can create a static home page, or you can have it so that your most recent posts are listed on the home page, as many bloggers do.

How you set up your blog will depend on your niche and what you want to achieve.

A Blogger blog is easy to set up and use and there's a plethora of information online to help you.

Although many people say it's more professional to have your own blog or website, if you do decide to set up a Blogger blog, it is possible to have it under your own domain name later if you change your mind.

If you're at all unsure about creating your own website or messing about with hosting or you just want to get started quickly, blogger.com is a great option.

Some people on the internet say that your site will look unprofessional if you use a free blog on blogger.com. But I disagree.

I think that because blogger.com is owned by Google, your site will show up in the search results more often than if you have any other type of website.

Whenever I'm surfing the net, blogger blogs always show up in Google's search results and often on the first page of results, and this is because Google likes to index its own blogs. So I think that having a blogger.com website, is more of a help with getting your site in front of more people rather than a hindrance, and it's only seen as being unprofessional, by internet snobs.

But however you choose to create your first website, just remember to keep it simple, or as it's better known, KISS (Keep It Simple Stupid).

You need a site that's easy to maintain, simple to add content to and that opens quickly when people visit. You don't want to be messing around with flashy banners that don't work or videos or images that are so large they dominate every page.

You want a site that's easy on the eyes, simple to navigate and has so much useful information that people not only want to visit again and again, but they also Tweet about it and link to pages on your site to share it with others.

Protecting Your Private Information Online

One of the great things about the internet is that it's so public. You won't find a wider audience for your work. On the other hand one of the bad things about the internet is that it's so public.

What you put on your website is up to you, so if you want to include your address and telephone number you can (but I really, REALLY wouldn't advise it).

But no matter how much you try and keep this private information private, there is an online database that lists who owns each website and also includes their address and phone number.

This is called the WHOIS registry and ALL websites get listed here.

When you sign up for a website, you have to give your hosting company your private information (address, phone number, email address, etc.) and all this is entered in the WHOIS registry.

So how do you protect your private information?

I do it two ways.

With some of my websites, when I register a domain name and buy a hosting package, sometimes I ask for privacy protection. This usually has to be paid for but it's really cheap, I think it's around $15/year. What happens when you enable privacy protection is that the hosting company, or a privacy protection company employed on your behalf, will use their contact information in the WHOIS registry instead of yours.

Another thing I do with some of my other websites is use disposable information. By disposable I mean I use a PO box for my address and my phone number is a disposable one. It's a cell phone number and if it gets used and abused I just have to destroy the sim card and buy another. I have a cheap cell phone that has the disposable number and I don't use it for anything else. That way no one has my private cell phone number or my home number. And the email address is simply an email address from one of my websites and not my private email address.

That's how I protect myself online and unless you don't mind the whole world knowing your home address and phone number, you need to protect your private information too.

If you have a Blogger.com blog, your information doesn't get entered into the WHOIS database. Google is listed as the owner of all Blogger blogs.

How to Write Web Page Content Even If You Don't Know How

Every website needs content. You can't get away from it.

As a writer, I already have an edge on this one because I can write all my own content (and I've even written content for other people's websites too).

But what if you feel you can't write? What do you do then? We'll go through your options of how to create online content. But first we'll look at how to get visitors to you website using your content.

First of all, the internet runs on links. You have to have links to your website from search engines and from other websites so that people can find your site.

The easiest way to do that is by using SEO, Search Engine Optimisation. This means using key words and key phrases in your web page content so that anyone searching online for that type of information will easily find yours.

For example, if you're writing about growing vegetables and you know that people might be using the phrase "how to grow vegetables" to search Google, then you need to get these words into your website without it looking too obvious. So you could use those exact words as a heading for a page of content, or you can slip it into what you're writing like "a lot of people don't know how to grow vegetables...". I know that is a cheesy example but I'm keeping it simple to get my point across.

If you don't know what people are searching for in your niche/topic you can use a search tool to find out. Just go to Google's free AdWords Keyword Planner at https://adwords.google.com/KeywordPlanner and search for different key words and key phrases.

Click on 'Tools' in the top menu, and then choose 'Keyword Planner' and from there you can start adding words and phrases. Once you click 'search' it will bring back not only the words you're searching for, but also a hundred other related search terms. It will also show you how many people search for it in a month, how much competition there is for it and other statistics as well.

From this information you can decide what's popular, what's TOO popular and what's not popular at all. And by too popular, I mean for some keywords there are so many competing websites that yours will never show up in Google's search results. Let's face it, when you search on Google for information, do you ever go past the 1st or 2nd page of results? Not many people do. That's why it's sometimes better to find key words with less competition to start with so that your website shows up on the first few pages of search results rather than thousands of pages later.

You will have to open an account with Google to use this Keyword Planner, but it's free to do. But don't put in your credit card information when you begin to use the keyword planner. Instead click the link to skip that step.

The best place to put your keywords is in your headings or subheadings on your web pages and in the first paragraph.

Web page content isn't all about what you write on the page but also how it looks. People don't want to read through lengthy text online. So instead break your pages up with images, white space, sub headings and bulleted lists. It makes it more appealing to the eyes and easier to read. Also make sure your font is large enough so that people don't have to squint to read.

And if you don't know how to write your own content here are a few ideas that can help you create it more easily.

Instead of typing, you could speak what you have to say into a voice recorder and then transcribe it later. If you're anything like me, as soon as a voice recorder is switched on, you stumble and bumble through what you want to say. I even struggle with leaving voice messages on people's phones.

But the good thing about recording what you want to say, is that no one else has to hear it and you can leave out all the ums and ahhs and all the long silences. And once your words are written up you'll be surprised at how professional it reads.

Another way to make writing easier is to go online, collect a few articles from other websites, copy and paste the bits you want into a text document, and from there, write it all out in your own words.

Remember, it's illegal to copy someone else's work and put it on your website. That's called copyright infringement and your website can be shut down by your hosting company if someone complains.

So never EVER copy someone else's writing. By all means take their ideas and write them up in your own way, but don't outright copy what they've written.

If you want to find articles that are free to use, try an article directory site such as http://www.ezinearticles.com. They have millions of articles, all written by different people. And with an article directory, all the articles are free to republish. All you have to do is agree to keep the article 'as is' with no changes and include the author's information with it.

The only problem with doing this is that the search engines don't like what they call 'duplicate content' so if they find the same article on multiple websites, they'll only index one of them in the search results, and it's usually the first site where the article appeared.

So while these articles are free to use, it's still better to collect a few together, create a patchwork of information from them all and then write it up in your own words. It won't take long to do and the search engines will come over all warm and cuddly when they see original content on your site.

Another option for getting content for your site is to buy PLR articles. PLR stands for Private Label Rights. These types of articles are sold on the internet with no copyright restrictions. This means that you can buy a set of articles and do with them whatever you want. You can publish them on your website just as they are or change them or rewrite them in any way at all.

I won't give you a link to PLR articles online because there are so many different places you can get these from and they are usually sold in packs of articles per niche. So if you are going to buy articles about sky diving, you'd have to Google "PLR sky diving articles" or something similar to find where the correct niche articles are.

And if you buy PLR articles and you don't want to rewrite them yourself you can always pay someone else to do it for you by hiring someone through a freelance website such as upwork.com You can find all kinds of freelancers here including writers, editors, software designers, website designers and even lawyers. You can also sign up yourself and sell your skills.

I sometimes use upwork.com to get work done for me. It's usually things I cannot do myself or something that I can do but it takes me so long that it's far easier to pay someone else to do it.

You can also use Upwork to hire someone to write your website content from scratch, but you need to be explicit about what you want so that there is no misunderstanding between you and the person you hire.

Of course, if your website/blog is more personal than professional, it should be easy to write content for it yourself because you're just taking what's in your head and pouring it onto the page.

It's a well known 'secret' among writers that the easiest way to write is by using WAYS.

WAYS is an acronym for Write As You Speak. So write as though you are speaking. That's what I've done throughout this ebook. I just think about what I want to say and then write it down exactly as it is in my mind.

In my head it's like a conversation going on and that's how it needs to come across on the page, because that's what makes it easy to read.

So when you're writing, just imagine that you're speaking out loud to a friend, and write down exactly how it sounds in your head. Or alternatively, you can actually speak as you write, that way you'll know how well it reads. Sometimes it's all to easy to write something and think that it's okay, but when you read it out loud it sounds ridiculous.

Sometimes when I'm writing, I notice that my lips are moving at the same time as though I'm talking what I'm writing. But I always assume that's a good thing because I often get emails from people saying that they like my writing style or that my articles and ebooks are so easy to read.

If you write as you speak you shouldn't go far wrong with writing web page content.

Chapter 8.

Selling Physical and Digital Products

Having a product/s to sell on the internet is the best way to make money online. We'll be looking later at how to make money online when you don't have a product to sell, but for now we'll be discussing selling physical and digital products (either yours or someone else's).

If you have your own products you can be completely in control of where they're sold, how much they sell for and who you allow to help you sell them.

There are only two types of products that are sold online. Physical products and digital products. Physical products need to be packed and shipped whereas digital products can be uploaded to the internet and customers can download copies of it automatically with no extra effort on your part needed.

Some people sell services online (such as consulting) but that is a whole other topic and doesn't provide a true LLS.

Selling Physical Products

If you have a skill or talent for creating physical products and that is what you want to sell then that's great. But depending on the size and weight of what you're selling, it can interfere with where you work. If you sell small light items, you can pack some in your suitcase and travel anywhere. On the other hand if you're selling large, heavy objects, you can only store them in one place.

You can simplify selling physical products by using what's called a drop shipping wholesale company to deal with the physical side of packing and posting your products. Of course you'd have to pay them to store your products, so it's better to see how big your business grows before you look into this type of company.

But if you're going to start a business about knitting or something similar and you plan to sell what you make, then it could be better to keep a small stock and create the products on an as-ordered basis, providing, of course, that you're up front with customers about how long it will take to produce what they've ordered.

If you are planning to sell physical products, no doubt you already know exactly what you're going to sell and how you're going to do it. You might set up payment links for customers using PayPal or perhaps you're going to set up an eBay account or use another similar auction site.

If you want to know more about using drop-shipping companies and eBay, it's easy to Google this information.

It's also really easy to find products to buy online in bulk so that you can sell them on to your customers.

For instance, I once thought of selling Buddhist items on eBay. I thought of starting with selling prayer bead necklaces. So I Googled "mala necklaces wholesale" and it came back with around 678,000 results. So then I changed it to "mala necklaces wholesale in Australia" and it came back with over 368,000 results and it seems that I could buy them in bulk for as little as $1 or $2 each, and sell for up to 10 times that amount.

So then I looked at eBay and how to set up a whole eBay store. I figured that I could have set the whole thing up in just a couple of days once my stock arrived.

But I got busy with my other online businesses and never did see it through. But it just goes to show how simple it would have been to buy stock and then take photos of it all and set it up in an eBay store.

Or I could have put the photos on a website or blog of my own and set up an online store using PayPal, which is the payment processor that eBay uses.

I once made money online selling used books on Amazon. I lived in the UK at the time and I went around buying up used books, especially ex-stock from libraries, and selling them through Amazon.

I discovered that I could buy these books for only 50 pence or a pound and resell them online for 10 to 20 pounds, plus the customers paid the postage and Amazon provided the address labels.

It worked well for a while but it did mean that I had to run to the post office every 2 days (Amazon gave me 48 hours to ship the books) plus I had to bulk-buy cardboard book packaging that easily wrapped around the books, but it wasn't expensive.

But it wasn't a full-time income, although I did do quite well with it, until I moved back to Australia and so far Amazon is new here and doesn't yet allow the sale of used books (at this time of writing). But maybe I'll sell used books again when it does.

As I mentioned earlier, drop shipping is another way to sell physical products online, even products you don't own.

I've never done it myself, but how it works is that you advertise another company's products on your website (or products from several different companies) and you get paid a commission for every sale.

One of the biggest problems with working this way, is that if the product isn't delivered on time, the customers complain to you because it's you that they bought the product from.

And what the companies want from you is for you to heavily promote their products, but they do help you with keeping your data base up to date (with changes in stock and what is currently out of stock, new in stock, etc) and they usually allow you to use their images of their stock.

Selling Digital Products

Selling digital products is easy because you can set up the buying process, and customers can buy and download copies of your product automatically.

Digital products come in the form of ebooks or similar text based products, digital images, and software.

If you have a great idea for a digital product but don't know how to create it yourself, you can hire someone from a freelancing website, as discussed before, to create it for you. Of course this could be costly, depending on what your idea is, but if you think it will be a good seller then it could be worth the investment.

If you're going to produce text based products like ebooks, you need to format them into a PDF document. This makes them easy to download and, if you add security settings, it makes it harder for people to copy it.

You can download free software from the internet that will turn any text document into a PDF file. You can download Cute PDF software from www.cutepdf.com/. This type of free software is easy to use but it's limited in what it can do. For instance, you cannot set any security to your files.

PDF ebooks are popular because they can be read on any computer.

These days both Word for Windows and Pages for Mac have "save as PDF" as an option.

Ebooks that are read on ebook readers such as the iPad, the iPhone, the Nook, Kobo and Sony Reader are known as .epub files. .epub files are basically html files, which allows them to be read on virtually any screen reader.

To make sure a file converts well to an .epub file, it has to have simple formatting. You can read more detailed information about this at http://blog.bookbaby.com/2011/11/formatting-your-work-for-ebook-distribution/.

Pages software for Mac computers now come with an "export to ePub" option and you can even publish your ebook on Apple's iBook store straight from your computer.

If you have dreams of writing and selling ebooks on Amazon.com, you need to go to http://kdp.amazon.com and register for an account. You can then upload your ebook manuscript as a HTML file and Amazon will convert it into a Kindle ebook (which is different from an .epub file) for free. But again the formatting must be kept simple.

Amazon Kindle accounts are free to open and Amazon takes a percentage of every sale. You can download Amazon's free ebook "Building Your Book For Kindle" to help you with formatting.

You can now also use Kindle to sell your ebook as a print book too.

If you want to sell ebooks in more online stores, http://www.smashwords.com can also convert your manuscript into an ebook file for free and help you sell you ebook through more online ebook stores including Apple iBooks and Barnes & Noble ebook store.

If you need a 3D cover for your ebook (similar to the one I have for this ebook) you can get one made in just a couple of days for about $35 (with images supplied) from CoversCorp. This website is run by a guy called Buddy, and while English doesn't seem to be his first language, if you can get past the bad grammar on his website, you'll soon see that he is brilliant at what he does.

He can also provide you with a web page to match your ebook cover. Even if you don't want an ebook cover or a web page designing, it's worth it just to go to his website and look at his portfolio to see how good his work is.

But if you are going to sell digital products from your website then you need to have plenty of ideas about what they are going to be. You need to sit down (again) and brain storm exactly what types of products you can create, or have created for you.

But selling ebooks online, or any other type of text-based products, all comes back down to needing to have the talent to write. So if you can't write an ebook, then what else can you do?

We'll be looking at how you can make money from your website when you don't have a product at all to sell. And believe it or not, there are already thousands of people all over the world making money this way.

But when you are creating your own digital products, particularly when it's an ebook or similar product, make sure that all your words are your own. Don't copy what someone else has already done. Even if you only copy a part of what someone has already written this is known as plagiarism, and it is illegal and you could get sued in court or lose your website, or both.

And even if neither happen, you can lose your good reputation and once that's gone, it's irrevocably gone. If someone begins complaining online that you've stolen their work, this bad news will go viral (bad things always do on the internet).

And it needn't be the original author who complains. If anyone surfing the internet sees someone else's work on a website (or in an ebook) where it shouldn't be, all they have to do is write about it on their website and then everyone in the whole world will know. This type of publicity you don't want. And not only that, stealing someone else's work is just plain rotten.

Outsourcing is a very easy way to get products made for you. But I would advise that if you are creating a large product, like an ebook, to get more than one person to help with it. This is because, if you only pay one person to do it, and their work isn't good, then it's too late by the time they've completed the whole project for you.

It would be wiser to get several people to produce shorter pieces of work for you so that you can try them out first. I've heard dreadful stories over the years of people who have outsourced large writing projects to an unknown person, only to find that they couldn't write, or their first language wasn't English and that they had secured the job by getting someone with better writing skills to write their proposal for them.

Once you do create your own digital product then it's time to start selling it.

But how do you do that?

The easiest and quickest way is to open an account with PayPal.com. PayPal is one of the oldest online payment companies on the internet. With Paypal you can open a business account and use their resources to set up "Buy Now" links so that anyone who wants to buy your product can click the link and be taken to the PayPal website to finish their purchase.

Of course once they've paid they need to be able to download what they've bought. That's why you also need to create a download page that contains a link to the product. When you set up a "Buy Now" link it does prompt you to provide a link to your download page which is where PayPal will redirect customers after their purchase.

Once you've set up your sales page with a "Buy Now" link and your download page, you're then free to leave it to take care of itself. And using PayPal means that not only can customers buy your products through their own PayPal account, but PayPal also takes most major credit cards too.

Another way to sell your products online is through online networks. These networks also give you the option of also allowing affiliates to sell your products, if you want them to.

Affiliates are people who sell other people's products for a commission. And affiliate networks are websites that allow many different companies to sell their products all through the one website.

One of the biggest online networks is Commission Junction (now called Conversant) at http://cj.com. Commission Junction sells physical and digital products from hundreds of different companies.

The largest digital online network is ClickBank.com. They have over 100,000 affiliates and over 20,000 digital products.

Another online network is e-junkie.com. They also sell thousands of digital products and have a huge army of affiliates. But with this website vendors are responsible for paying their own affiliates, unlike ClickBank and Commission Junction, who take care of that for you.

And of course, there are many other online networks right across the internet. You only have to Google your niche and the words "affiliate program" or "affiliate network" to find more. My favourite though, is E-Junkie.com for selling my PDF ebooks.

Another good thing about E-Junkie, is that you can upload your products to their website which is where your customers download them from. So if you have a free Blogger blog and you cannot upload your own ebooks to it, you can use E-Junkie instead.

Having your ebooks on the E-Junkie website is also more secure than having them on your own site. And you can upload up to 10 digital products on one account for a low fee of $5/month (that amount was correct at time of writing). They also let you set up a sales page for each of your products on their site too.

I find with my products, that I sell most of them myself and not through an affiliate, apart from the super affiliates who pop up now and again and promote one of my products. Then the sales start to grow at a rapid rate. But either way it suits me because even the affiliates who don't make sales or make very few, are still out there promoting my products, and I love this kind of free marketing.

Do Your Research

Before you decide to go out and launch your own product, make sure you do a bit of online research first. You need to know what similar products are already being sold.

Once you find them look at how good or how bad you think they are. Notice what you think is missing from them and then go and create something better. If you find that all the other products are lacking in some way that yours isn't, use this as your USP (Unique Selling Proposition).

There is a lot of competition already on the internet for whatever you decide to sell, so you need yours to be different. You need yours to be much better than the rest. And then you need to use your product's uniqueness to outsell the others.

And Then There Was More

Don't just stop at creating one product. Your business needs to be ongoing and so does your product creating.

I am always on the lookout for my next big ebook idea. I'm a writer so the products I create, apart from websites, are always books and ebooks.

No matter what else I'm doing, I always seem to spot a potential idea to expand on and make money. Even when I'm watching TV, something someone says, or the way something is advertised can sometimes spark an idea that I'll mull over for a few days or weeks.

Other times ideas just simply come to me when I least expect it. I can be vacuuming, dog walking, gardening, or even reading a book. And all of a sudden an idea will come to me as though out of nowhere. It can seem really random, but there it is. That's when I run and grab my ideas notebook and write down what I've thought about.

And usually, once I start writing an idea down, more and more ideas about it keep coming so I write down as much as I can because, I know that as soon as I stop writing, I'll forget most of what I just thought.

Then weeks or even months later, if I've forgotten about it, I might come across it and read all my notes and get enthusiastic about it all over again.

So wherever you are and whatever you're doing, keep looking for ideas in everything you see and do.

Selling products is a numbers game in the end. The more products you have to sell, the more money you can make.

If you have just one product and you can sell 10 a day that's good (depending on the price). But if you have 10 products and you can sell 10 of each a day then that's 10 times more income.

Handling Refunds

Now and again you'll come across someone who's not happy with what they've bought from you and they'll ask for a refund.

What I do is refund their money immediately. I don't quibble and I don't ask questions. If someone's asking for their money back then they're probably angry, because no one wants to buy something and be disappointed with it.

Customers who are dissatisfied with what they've bought and get a prompt refund are happy customers. People are more satisfied if something goes wrong with their purchase and it's fixed immediately than customers who have bought something and nothing went wrong.

Good customer service is everything. It can sometimes be even more important than the products you're selling.

Keep your customers satisfied, no matter what. And whether you think they deserve a refund or not, just give them a refund.

Chapter 9.

How To Make Money When You Don't Have Anything To Sell

Making money online is a lot easier if you have something to sell.

But what if you're not creative or crafty but you still want to live the laptop lifestyle? How do make money online?

There are actually millions of people online with no product of their own, but they're all making money, and some of them make up to half a million dollars a year. Just check out Rosalind Gardner's Super Affiliate Handbook to see what I mean.

These people are called affiliate marketers. They make money by promoting other people's products for a commission.

In the last chapter we looked at how affiliates can help you sell your products, and on the flip side, you can become an affiliate and start selling other people's products yourself.

But you still need a niche website. It's no good having a site that sells anything and everything. There are websites like that (Amazon.com is one of them) but not many can get away with that.

It's far easier (and that's what the laptop lifestyle is all about) to stick to one niche and sell related products from your website.

But that doesn't mean you'll only be selling one type of product.

For instance, I have a website for freelance writers so I spend a lot of time promoting writing courses. But I also promote stationary, computers, software and other related products.

Even if you have a simple website related to your hobby you can still promote a whole range of products. So if you have a website about gardening, you could promote seeds, potting mix, gardening tools, gardening magazines, gardening books, fences, sheds, and even promote the services of landscape gardeners.

Once you begin your website you'll find more ideas about what to promote as you go along.

And even if you have your own products to sell, you can still work as an affiliate at the same time and promote other people's products as well, as long as they don't compete with yours.

Making Money With Affiliate Programs.

Affiliate marketing has been a common way for people to make money online for years now. There are even people known as super affiliates earning up to half a million dollars a year promoting other people's products online.

Of course super affiliates promote mostly what are known as high ticket items, meaning what they promote brings in high commissions. For example, if you wanted to earn a high commission, and your website is about health and fitness, you could promote treadmills costing up to $6,000 each, and if someone made a purchase through your affiliate link, even if you are only earning 10% commission, just one sale could earn you $600. And you don't need many sales like this to earn a high income.

You can find high paying affiliate programs at http://www.highpayingaffiliateprograms.com.

When you search online you can find thousands of affiliate programs run by thousands of different companies. But having too many affiliate accounts isn't a good thing.

Firstly, it takes a lot more time to keep promoting products from too many different places. You have to keep logging in to different accounts and have to keep track of which product is from which company.

Secondly, affiliate sales usually have to reach a certain amount of money before companies pay you, so if you're only promoting a couple of products from one company, it may be a while before you accumulate enough money in your account to get paid.

To do it the easy way, it's better to sell products from multiple companies through an affiliate network. This way, it doesn't matter which company you sell products for, because your earnings will accumulate in one account (the network's account) and so you can get paid sooner, and you can keep track of all your affiliate promotions from one place.

One of the biggest affiliate networks online is Commission Junction. They have thousands of products from hundreds of different companies all over the world. You can search their site by category or by advertiser, join as many programs as you want, and then use the banners and links provided to help advertise products.

Another huge online affiliate network is ClickBank.com. They have over 20,000 digital products and over 100,000 affiliates. Their commissions are also very high with some products paying 75%. One of the drawbacks of using ClickBank though is that some of the products are quite low quality so you have to be careful what you promote from there.

I usually buy a product from ClickBank before I promote it just to make sure I'm not promoting garbage. And because I've been working online for many years now, I also often get people emailing me and offering me a free copy of their product to see if I want to promote it for them.

I say yes, if it fits in with one of my niche sites. But if I don't like the product, I won't promote it. I also usually don't say anything negative about it online if I didn't like it. I just don't promote it and I tell the owner why.

I used to have ebooks on ClickBank that I sold myself. Sometimes I'd get emails from affiliates asking if they could have a free copy to see if they want to promote it. I'd usually say no, unless the affiliate is someone already known to me or they are already selling my ebooks and making sales. I'm all for letting them have a free copy to see if they can sell more, if they're a decent affiliate. But if I don't know them I say no to free copies.

I once had someone email me asking for a copy of one of my ebooks. I'd never heard of the person before, or their website. So I checked them out. I visited their website and saw that the content was badly written on every page and it was littered with links and banners to random products from ClickBank. Then I visited the WHOIS register and saw that their site had only been online for 7 days. Also the site was registered in a man's name, David, yet the person who emailed me was called Shirley.

So I investigated further. I looked at his (her?) web page source code on a page where they were advertising other ClickBank products, to see what his ClickBank ID was. Then I Googled his ClickBank ID and found that he had another website with that exact name as his ID. But this website was run by a man called David. This website also had badly written content, the same way that the other one did. So I went to Google Images and searched the woman's name he'd given me, and yeesh! The photos were of a man wearing thickly applied makeup and wearing a woman's blouse and a strange wig (at least I think it was a wig).

I had no idea what this guy David was up to but I didn't want any part of it. So I emailed back, told him that I knew he wasn't the woman he first claimed to be, that his website had only been online for a week and that most new affiliates buy ebooks to evaluate them and not ask for a free copy.

He wasn't very happy, to say the least. In fact he was quite verbally abusive. And I haven't heard from Shirley/David ever since.

So if you do start selling ebooks or other products through an affiliate network, look out for freebie chasers and don't give them anything.

And if you want to join the ClickBank affiliate program go to the home page at http://www.clickbank.com and click on "create account" at the top of the page.

Note: I no longer sell products on ClickBank after dissatisfaction of their new fee structure and refund policy.

Amazon has one of the oldest and biggest affiliate programs on the internet. Their commissions aren't high (usually around 4% to 6%) but they sell such an array of products that it's possible to earn a decent amount of money. That's because once a customer clicks on one of your affiliate links, it doesn't matter what they buy or how much they buy, you get the commission for every purchase.

I was reading online a few weeks ago about one guy who has a website about writing and only advertises books from Amazon. Yet he made a big commission after someone clicked through his affiliate link for a book and ended up buying a motor bike engine. I didn't even know Amazon sold motor bike engines.

If you want to join the Amazon affiliate program just go to the Amazon home page at http://amazon.com and click on the affiliate link at the bottom of the page. You can also affiliate to all the amazon sites worldwide.

One of the biggest affiliate networks on the internet is called VigLink.

Viglink is affiliated with hundreds and even thousands of other companies so when you sign up with Viglink, you get access to them all.

They supply affiliate links plus they also use PPC campaigns which means for some of their affiliated companies, you'll receive a payment when someone clicks on a link on your website, regardless of whether they make a purchase or not.

And with some of Viglink's affiliated companies that have thousands of products, you don't even need to put a link to it on your website. Just mention a product and Viglink will link automatically.

There is a lot more to Viglink, but it's so easy, and free, to sign up for an account with them and start earning money.

And their website explains it all in simple terms. To join their affiliate program just go to http://cheritonhousepublishing.com/affiliates.html where you'll find links to this and other affiliate programs.

Apple also has an affiliate program where you can sell products from all the different i-stores. The iTunes Store, App Store, iBookstore and Mac App Store feature millions of songs, thousands of apps for iOS and Mac, Hollywood movies to rent or buy, TV shows, music videos, games, audiobooks and ebooks, and free podcasts.

Find out more about their affiliate program (they have different programs in different countries) at https://www.apple.com/itunes/affiliates/.

If you want to find even more affiliate programs or affiliate networks it's easy to search using Google. Just search for your niche keyword plus "affiliate program" or something similar.

Affiliate programs are not hard to find. Just start looking and soon your mind will be boggled with all the choices available.

Promoting products online as an affiliate is known as affiliate marketing. And it takes much more than placing ads on your website to make decent money. If all you do is copy and paste ads and banners on your website, you probably will make money. But you won't make enough to live on.

You need to actively promote products in as many places as possible.

Some affiliates use classified online advertising. Personally I've never marketed this way for my own products or as an affiliate. But I do know of some marketers who have made good money this way.

In another chapter we'll be looking at advertising and you'll find plenty of ways to advertise your website, your products and your affiliate products.

Advertising is EVERYTHING. No one has made a lot of money from not advertising.

But advertising online doesn't have to cost a lot of money. In fact you'll discover that most of it can be done for free.

And I'll show you how to do it in the next chapter.

But first, we need to look at another way to earn money from your website when you have nothing of your own to sell.

Pay Per Click Advertising

PPC Advertising is another way to make money from any website.

And it does exactly what it says. It Pays Per Click. This means that any time someone clicks on one of the ads on your website, you earn money whether they buy anything or not.

The money can be anything from a couple of cents to several dollars. All you have to do is place a small piece of code on your website and the ads show up automatically. There's nothing more for you to do.

There are several different companies that offer PPC advertisement income but by far the biggest, best and easiest one to use is Google's AdSense program.

With AdSense, all you have to do is go to Google's home page, click on the link at the bottom that says "advertising" and click on AdSense (not AdWords). From there you can sign up for an Adsense account for free and begin placing PPC ads on your website once you're approved.

AdSense ads, or any PPC ads, are easy to use. You just choose the size and type you want (image ads, text ads or both, or ads that are 'responsive' and change to fit every screen size automatically), choose your ad colours for the text ads (this helps them fit in with the colour scheme of your website) and then you simply copy the piece of script that is provided and paste it into your webpage HTML source code.

If you have Google Blogger Blog, there is a widget especially made for placing AdSense ads on your blog which makes it even easier to do than usual.

Google will then display ads on your site that are relevant to your webpage keywords. Sometimes Google's algorithms get it a bit wrong, but eventually it figures things out. For example, I once wrote an article about being able to focus and get more writing done. When I first uploaded the web page, the AdSense ads that were displaying were all about the Ford Focus car. But after a couple of days I checked it again and the ads had gone back to being writing related.

If you have a WordPress blog, it's still possible to copy and paste the AdSense code into the source code. You have to find the source code through the editor link in your dashboard, then choose where you want to place the ad. If you want to display an ad in your sidebar, you'll have to find the source code for 'sidebar' and copy and paste it in there.

Just check how it looks once you've done it, and if it doesn't display correctly you can delete what you pasted and put it in the correct place. Just remember that new ad placements take up to 10 minutes to start displaying on your web page, so you may not be able to see them at first.

Google now also offers "automatic" ads so you don't even have to place to ads on your webpage yourself. Just upload one piece of code to your pages and Google automatically places ads for you.

If you want to make it easy to put AdSense ads on a WordPress blog, just do a Google search for "free wordpress theme" with "Adsense ready" or something similar.

A Word Of Warning...

Google are very particular about their AdSense ads. They don't like websites full of garbage information that only exist to make money from AdSense ads, and there are a lot of sites like this.

Some people, usually those whose first language isn't English, will put a blog online, cover it in AdSense ads and then use software that's called an "article spinner" to get content from other sites, "spin" it (this means the software - which is nothing more than a giant thesaurus - changes as many words as it can to something similar) to make it look like an original article.

Sadly, all this does is render the article as unreadable garbage. I came across one of these sites yesterday.

The "spun" text on the page was "Giving thoroughly over whatever website addicted to may tough. Most of us find that it's much harder inside kinds thanks to beneficial addictive style."

I tracked down the original article, which wasn't hard to do because it had the same title, and it was "Giving up anything that you are addicted to is hard. Some people find it harder than others due to an addictive personality."

Did you spot the difference?

If you ever see an ad for article spinning software, run a mile away. When I come across sites like this one, I click on the corner of the AdSense ad on the page, where it says "Ad Choices." That takes me to Google's AdSense complaints page where I report the site as a "spam" site. Google usually closes the website owners AdSense account within 48 hours.

I hate sites like that because they are a waste of my time visiting them so I always report them. And I'm not the only one reporting sites like this. So if you ever think you can have a junk website and live off AdSense income, don't do it.

Also Google has a requirement that if you place AdSense ads on your site, you must place a warning on your privacy page about the cookies these ads use to track visitors. So don't forget to do that (it's just a matter of copying and pasting the info they provide).

AdSense is a great way to make money. I earn money every day with Adsense. My writing websites don't earn much income from AdSense because they don't earn much per click - only a few cents most of the time. But it doesn't bother me because my other niche sites earn more AND it's only extra money, not my sole source of income. So the money Google pays me every month is great and it's all profit because it doesn't cost me anything to put the ads on my sites.

There are many people who earn their whole online income from AdSense ads. They just set up websites, update them all the time with great content, and rely on clicks on their ads to make money for them.

And if you get into the correct niche it can be very profitable. Some of the high paying ads can pay around $6 or $7 per click. Also websites in the travel niche tend to do very well with AdSense income because although the ads only pay around $2/click or less, it seems that people will click on just about anything when they're searching online to book a holiday.

Ebay also has a program called the Ebay Partner Program. You can read more about it at https://partnernetwork.ebay.com. Just like the Google AdSense program, you just copy and paste the script they provide onto your web page source code.

And although it's not a PPC program, as in, you don't get paid per click, it's similar because you only have to copy and paste the code they provide and eBay will provide advertisements for relevant products currently on eBay.

They also calculate Earnings Per Click in their affiliate reports so you can see how effective the ads are performing. That is why I've included it in this PPC section.

Not only that, but just like AdSense ads, they also monitor your visitors browsing history to display ads that they think are specifically relevant to that person, which can further increase clicks and sales. AND they provide Buy It Now buttons in their ads so that customers can make purchases straight away from your website.

There are many PPC companies online but it's best to stick to only using one or two so that your web pages don't look stuffed with ads.

Some of the PPC companies you can use are:

https://www.infolinks.com

http://www.bidvertiser.com/

https://www.revenuehits.com

PPC ads are the fastest way to start generating online income. In fact, if you can place PPC ads on your web pages straight away, and get plenty of traffic to your site the same day, it's possible that people coming to your site will click on an PPC ad as they leave. So you could earn some money before you even go to bed.

But never EVER click on ads on your own site. Not only will your PPC account be closed, but you'll forfeit any earnings. Clicking ads on your own site is called Click Fraud.

Chapter 10.

How to Sell Things Online

If you create a product to sell (or have an affiliate product that you're promoting), you need a sales page to sell it from. Tiny ads won't do it, especially if you want to allow affiliates to help you make sales. You have to have a sales page to direct customers to so that they can find out everything they need to know to make a purchase.

And 'everything they need to know' doesn't mean you have to tell them everything about your product. What you place on your sales page isn't an explanation of what you're selling, but rather the benefits the customer is going to receive once they buy your product.

You see the customer doesn't care about your product. They don't care what it looks like, they don't care what it can do. They only care about what it can do for them.

Now that may sound selfish, but just think about it. When you buy something, are you buying it because of what it can do, or because of what it can do for you?

Look at it this way: You wouldn't buy a lawn mower if you didn't need a new one. But if you saw a sales page for a lawn mower that was lightweight, easy to use and could cut your lawn mowing time in half while at the same time giving your lawn a manicured look, wouldn't you want to upgrade to that one? (Damn, I want one now, even though I know it doesn't exist because I just made it up!)

Look at it another way. Say you were thinking of buying a treadmill. If you saw an ad talking about how great the treadmill was, how fast it can go, how steep an incline it has, how many dials and gadgets it has; would you be tempted to buy it? Probably not.

But if you saw an ad for the same treadmill that talked about how fit you'd become, how easy it is to use, how you'll be trim in no time at all with very little effort, how the dials and other gadgets it has makes it so simple for you to watch exactly how well your progressing; wouldn't you be more inclined to buy it?

Now I'm no fitness expert (I hate gyms and I never run unless someone's chasing me), so I'm not entirely sure what makes people want to buy a treadmill. But I know that if they are, they want to know what it's going to do for them. These are called benefits and that's what customers are looking for. Describing what the treadmill has, are features. No one is interested in features.

A statement like "We've been in business for 20 years" is describing a feature. But saying "We've been in business for 20 years so you KNOW we are a company you can trust" is a describing a benefit to the customer.

So when you write a sales page, make sure it's full of benefits, not features.

To help you keep on track, every sales page should be able to answer what are known as the Money Questions. Whenever someone reads a sales page, whether they know it or not, they are subconsciously asking questions, and it's usually the same questions. And online sales pages are usually quite long so you must make sure what it contains is always answering the money questions.

So before you write your sales page, answer (in writing) the following questions:

- Why should I read this page?
- How are you going to help me?
- Why should I read the rest of this page?
- So what?
- Why should I care?
- What's in it for me?
- Why is what you're offering better than any other?
- Why should I believe you?
- What is it going to cost me?
- What's my risk?
- What happens next?

The next thing to do, after you've written your answers to all the above questions (and your answers can be as long as you want) you need to check what others are already doing with their sales pages for similar products and copy their ideas.

Look for sentences and phrases that show:

- What's important to the reader
- Feelings and emotions that the reader may have
- Situations/problems that the reader might be going through
- The effects of not solving the problem

And make sure that your sales page contains the same - but don't copy other people's words.

Next you need to create a lead headline. This is the most important part of your sales page because if the reader isn't interested in what your headline is offering, they won't bother to read any further.

Your lead headline has 3 things it must do:

- It must exploit the problem the reader is having
- It must show that there is a cure
- It must create a curiosity factor.

So if you're selling a cure for baldness, your lead headline might be, "Are You Sick and Tired Of Losing Your Hair? 9 Out Of 10 Men Said This New Treatment Works Fast!"

See? There's the problem, a cure and (hopefully) curiosity to find out what the new treatment is.

Next your lead paragraph needs to hit the reader over the head with a statement that shows that you really understand what's going on and that you can help them. It doesn't matter if all you're selling are pretty doilies. You need to show that you understand how important it is for them to own your doilies. Because if they think your doilies won't help them, they won't buy them.

So your lead paragraph needs to show that you understand what the reader's worst feeling/problem is that they have and that you know a solution that will make them the happiest.

The rest of the sales page should progress like a story that leads to a satisfying conclusion.

You can also give a true-to-life situation the reader can relate to, that illustrates that you understand their problem. Don't be too vague with this or use the wrong words. Speak their language, because this is where you earn their trust.

At the end you need to show the price of what you're selling and you must justify it. So if you're selling an air freshener that will take away smells, you can say "that's a small price to pay to have a fresh smelling home for weeks on end. And it's far cheaper than paying a professional company hundreds of dollars to come in and fix the problem for you."

Also make sure your price stands out and is easy to see. Many people will skim down the page to find the price before they start reading. So fill your sales page with plenty of eye-catching sub headings so price skimmers will see them on the way down and after finding the price, may come back up to read more.

Before and after the "buy now' link at the bottom of page, provide an extra paragraph or two that paints an idyllic picture of how improved their life will be once they've made their purchase.

If you do all this then it should be easy to make sales. You've given your customers plenty of reasons to keep reading your sales page. You've shown them exactly how bad life is without your product and how great it's going to be once they own it.

The only other thing to remember with a sales page is to use the words 'you,' 'your,' and 'you'll' a lot to make it sound as though they already own your product so by the time they get to the bottom of the sales page, they feel they need it to buy it because it's already theirs.

Remember, it's emotion that makes people buy so use it liberally in your sales page.

Chapter 11.

Advertising

Nothing sells without advertising. All the big companies know this, that's why they never stop advertising. McDonalds have been running ads for years on TV, radio, billboards, magazines, bus stops and many other places besides. Why? Because nothing sells without advertising.

So if a big company like McDonald's knows they need to advertise all the time, so should you.

Because, if no one knows your product or website is there, you'll never make any money.

Everything you do online should be some form of advertising.

So how do you do it?

All the content you write for your website, even if it's just an information article, is advertising. It's advertising what a great website you have. Good web page content is one of the best kinds of advertising of all.

If people visit your site and like what they read, they'll be back. They'll also tell other people about your site and place links to your content on their website. You see this happening all the time on the internet, especially on social media.

In your content you should also provide links to other sites, especially sites that get a lot of traffic (visitors).

Why?

In your website control panel, you can look at your website stats and see not only what page on your site people are visiting the most, but also where visitors are coming from. So when someone visiting your site clicks on a link to another site, that link will show up in the other sites website stats. This lets them know that your website exists. And if you send them a lot of traffic through your link, they might check you out and even link back to your site.

Also the search engines like to see links to important websites. These are often called Authority Websites. It makes you look as though you know what you're talking about if you content links to an authority site.

SEO (Search Engine Optimisation) that we talked about before, is another type of advertising. You want your web pages to show up on the first page of Google search results. And Google does index pages, not sites. So every single page on your website needs to contain the correct keywords and key phrases in order for Google to rank your website higher than all the others and place it on the number 1 search results page.

Some people believe, and I think they are mostly right, that you don't need to worry about SEO too much. If you write useful content, the keywords and phrases should show up naturally on your pages anyway.

Personally, I don't fuss too much about SEO. I try and put keywords in my headings, but that's about all. And my sites rank pretty well. I'm living The Laptop Lifestyle, not the push and shove world of always wanting to make more money as fast as possible and worrying about every little detail in case I miss a tiny opportunity.

I write my web page content for people first and search engines second. I like my content to be readable rather than keyword stuffed. And it's always worked for me.

Article Marketing

This is one of the oldest and most used way of advertising for free on the internet.

The idea is that you write an article. At the end of your article you include an author's resource box that contains things like, "To read more visit http://...". You then submit the article to an article directory

Most article directories allow other website owners to publish your article on their website for free, provided that they include your resource box at the end.

This helps to advertise your website all over the internet. Article directories also usually have a huge email list of website owners looking for articles in certain niches, so if your article fits their niche they'll get your article emailed to them.

I must say that I'm a big fan of article marketing. My articles that I've submitted to article directories years ago are still generating visitors to my sites and are still being republished on other sites.

Marketing articles don't need to be very long, usually only about 400 to 700 words. But in my own experience, I find my longer articles of around 1,000 words or more, get republished more than my shorter articles.

Some people say it depends on which niche you're in as to whether short or longer articles work better. I personally think that if people are looking for information then they will prefer a longer article.

But in the end the choice is entirely yours. Article directories usually allow articles up to 2,000 words long, but that may be too many words for a free article. It's better to write a shorter (teaser) marketing article for the directories, and let the reader click through to read the rest of the information on your website.

Another thing to remember is that article directories only want links in your resource box to your website's home page, or to another page on your site. So you can't direct readers to an affiliate link.

The way around this is to say in your resource box, "You can find more information at http://www.mywebsite.com..." Make this a link to a longer article on the same subject at your website and include an affiliate link in it. Of course, replace the URL above with your own website address.

You can, of course, usually put a link in your marketing article to your own product or ebook sales page.

Make sure that your marketing articles contain usable information. No one wants to read a useless article, and people will judge you on your free content. So make sure that your marketing articles really knock people's socks off so that they'll be dying to go to your website and read more.

There are thousands of article directories online where you can submit articles for free. You can see a list of the top 50 at http://www.vretoolbar.com/articles/directories.php. My favourite directory is ezinearticles.com.

Article directories used to be amazing at getting visitors to your site because they ranked well in search results.

That was until Google decided that directories had too many spammy articles and so refused to index them any more.

But this doesn't matter to me because I still get plenty of visitors coming to my sites from ezinearticles.com and my articles still get republished on other websites.

Obviously, it's not as effective as it used to be but it still works well for me and because less people write articles for them it means less competition.

There are also article directories that don't allow reprints of articles. They are more of an article bank, where articles are stored for everyone to read.

So how do you make money from article banks?

Most of them use Google Adsense ads on their website and they display your Google ads some of the time and their own Google ads the rest of the time. These sites are usually quite heavily trafficked so Adsense earnings can do well. It's also a good way to get yourself known in more places.

Hubpages.com is one such site that operates this way. The accounts that people create are called hubs and their articles show up all the time in Google search results. You can read more about HubPages at http://jimmythejock.hubpages.com/_laptoplifestyle/hub/How-to-Earn-from-Hubpages.

Advertising in Blogs

Using other people's blogs is another free and easy way to advertise.

Nearly all blogs allow comments. And all comments have a link to the commenter's website.

Now this can work really well if you leave useful comments and don't spam. By spam I mean leaving a comment like "Nice blog. I'll visit again." I get these all the time on my blog. I hate it when people do that. I just mark it as spam so that the blog software knows to spam any other comments from them without bothering me to moderate it.

Blog comments can work in more ways than just provide a link to your website from your comment box. A couple of times, I've left a comment on someone's blog and they've reused it as a testimonial on another page. And I don't mind them doing this at all, if they link to my website.

This has also happened to me when I've sent an email thanking someone for something (a service or product) they did for me. I email them to say how great I thought they've done, and they publish it on their website as a testimonial, with a link to my website.

If you're good at writing, you can also look for blogs that allow guest blog posts. Just Google blogs in your niche and see if they have or allow guest bloggers.

If they do, write a post, following their guidelines (and they will have guidelines if they allow guest posts) and email it to them.

But your post has to be good. Make sure the content is:

- Relevant
- Useful
- Immediate (contains ideas readers can use straight away)

Guest blog posts can be the best kind of advertising because bloggers looking for guest posts will also have an email list of thousands of subscribers. So all their subscribers will see your post.

Advertising with Forums

There are a lot of people who swear by using forums for advertising, but I'm not one of them.

They say that if you join a forum or two in your niche and start replying to threads or start threads, then people will get to know and trust you and eventually you can add a link to your website or product in your signature and it won't look like advertising at all.

And while all this may or may be not be true, the problem that I have with forums is they take up a lot of your time, if you stay active on them. And for your advertising to look like your not advertising at all, you'd have to be pretty active on the forums.

I once read in an ebook that you only need to visit forums for an hour a day to make your advertising successful. An hour a day? Who has that much time to waste? Not me.

I've also found that there can be quite a few negative people on forums, the types who seem to exist only to upset other people. And they are a big waste of time to get into a discussion with.

But if you want to try forums for advertising, that's okay, because if you enjoy that kind of thing then you'll probably do well at it.

Advertising With Social Media

Social media is great for advertising.

I've set up my emails accounts so that whenever I write a new blog post it automatically gets published on Twitter. And I've set up my Twitter account so it posts my Tweets to my FaceBook page.

I'm not a real social media person but I do post to these sites every week and my blog posts get sent out to them too.

The easiest one to use IMHO is Twitter because it's so quick to Tweet something and I can share webpages I like so easily using Safari's quick "share" app.

I also use social media to brag about all my latest ebooks and affiliate products.

To date, I'm not a Pinterest user because my type of work (being a writer) doesn't involve needing lots of images, but it would be different if I had a food or craft website.

I've heard it said that it's best to put things on your website that people on Facebook like to share, but not everything can fit into that category.

I have found though, that memes are popular and get shared a lot. These are images that also have a motivational quote on them or a funny saying.

If you love using any social media site you can DEFINITELY use it to help you make money online.

Just remember that these sites are really for socialising and not for selling so don't go using blatant sales pitches all the time - or at any time for that matter.

But do share other people's posts, your own blog posts and anything else that will keep people interested and curious to know more about you.

Social media can really help drive sales if you do it subtly.

They say that before anyone buys a product from you, you have to get it in front of them at least 7 times. And a lot of the time this is true. I can advertise the same product to my list of email subscribers for years on end and one by one they keep buying. And social media can help with this 7-times rule too, if you keep it social.

I don't have any links to my social media accounts on my websites because I want to use social media to send people TO my sites, and not to send my website visitors to my social media accounts.

Search Engine Submissions

When you first create your website it's important to put it in front of the search engines to let them know it's there.

Some believe that search engine submissions aren't important, but if it's not important to the search engines then who is it important to?

Search engines like Google, spider the internet all the time looking for new pages on every website. They seem to favour sites that have new pages added to them on a regular basis rather than sites that are static and never change.

But they won't spider your site if they don't know it's there. They can always find your new pages because there's always a link to them from other pages. But a new site that no one knows about doesn't have any links to it anywhere.

That's why it's important to let the search engines know your site exists.

You can submit it to each search engine manually. Just Google "submit website to Google" then find the link to the submissions page, fill out your website information, and then repeat it all again for every other search engine.

The fast way I do it, is to use Submit Express. This is a website that will submit your website to several different search engines for you for free (scroll down their page to find the free option). It does say on their website that they'll submit your site to over 70 search engines, but I didn't even know that there were so many search engines. But it doesn't matter to me anyway. Their free service is a quick and easy way to submit a website.

After submitting your site, each of the search engines that your site is submitted to will hound you with emails, but all you have to do is unsubscribe using the link at the bottom of the emails.

I use Submit Express every time I create a new website because I like their service. It's fast and it's free. And most importantly, it works.

Email Advertising

There's a saying that 'the money is in the list' and I find that it's true.

If you have a website then you MUST use email for marketing and advertising.

When someone visits your website, even if they bookmark it, chances of them returning often, are zero.

That's why you need to put an email sign-up box on your website so that you can send marketing emails to your list as often as you want.

Of course, your emails won't look like marketing. They'll just look like emails. But each one will have some kind of link to something you're selling, or a link back to your website so that hopefully your readers will look around and either make a purchase or, at the very least, click on a PPC ad.

I have several email lists. One list I send a newsletter to every month, one list receives automatic blog updates (every time I create a new blog post my list is sent the post automatically) while the others all receive updates to my websites. Every time I write a new page of content, I email my list with a link to come and read it.

Does it help me to make sales? Yes it does. I don't know if it helps me to make more sales than any other type of advertising, but it is good for immediate sales. This means that when I create a new product, I send out several emails to my list and wham! I can make anything from a dozen sales to a hundred.

As an example, I once wrote an ebook. I emailed my list about it and offered a subscriber only discount. The ebook was going to be sold for $39 a copy. I offered it to my list first before it went on general sale for only $19, but for one week only. I can't remember the exact number of people that bought a copy but it was about 30. And at $19 each that's around $500. And at the time my subscriber list was very small. I had less than 200 subscribers.

The immediate income that email marketing can generate is always appreciated. It can take weeks to write an ebook (in amongst all the other work I do) and all the time I'm writing it, I'm not getting paid. That's why it's nice to finally reap a big chunk of the financial benefit quickly once it's finished.

Now I have thousands of subscribers altogether with all my websites and all my email lists, so now my immediate income from email marketing has increased significantly.

But for your emails to be effective you need to make sure that they get read. Simply emailing your list and bragging that you've got something to sell, won't work.

Instead your emails need to have an intriguing subject line and the content must be:

- Relevant
- Useful
- Immediate (useable straight away)
- Anticipated

You may have noticed that this bulleted list is almost identical to the one in the previous chapter. But this list has one added word. Anticipated. Emails must be anticipated. When someone sees there's an email from you in their inbox, they need to be eager to read it, knowing that whatever it contains will be something they want to read. Something that they can do. Something that will help them.

For my email lists I use an emailing company to deliver emails for me. I need one that is a trusted company that allows me to email my lists whenever I need to. I use double opt-in emails for all my lists. This means that when someone subscribes, they immediately receive an email asking if it was them that subscribed and telling them to click a link to confirm. And until they click the confirmation link in the email, they won't be subscribed.

I do this so that none of my emails can be accused of being spam. Every email sent also contains an unsubscribe link at the bottom so subscribers can opt out any time they want.

As mentioned earlier, I also send my blog posts to my blog subscribers automatically. The emailing software checks my blogs several times a day, and if there's a new post, they send it out.

They also provide sign up boxes. These boxes are easy to create by just choosing a box template and then I copy and paste the text into my source code and the box appears on the page.

If you have a blog you can use Google's free FeedBurner service to automatically send out an email every time you publish a post.

Sadly, FeedBurner is lousy at keeping the stats correct so you'll never be sure how many email subscribers you have.

But their service is free, reliable, simple to use and they even provide an email sign up box that you can put on your blog.

Blogs also have an RSS feed.

RSS stands for Real Simple Syndication and visitors can subscribe to this feed anonymously and your blog posts get delivered to their RSS feed reader.

One way to tempt more people to sign up for updates is to offer a free product to all new subscribers.

With an email service, when someone subscribes to my email list, they are automatically sent a "follow up" email that thanks them for subscribing and has a free ebook or two attached.

Sadly, this can't be done through FeedBurner.

I also use follow up emails to create a series of emails for extra marketing.

Using follow up emails means that I write a series of emails and schedule them to go out automatically either every day or every week. This means that whenever someone subscribes to that list, they automatically receive the emails in the order I scheduled them, over a set period of time.

I use this feature, which is often referred to as auto-responder emails, to do ongoing marketing for certain products.

For instance, if I'm selling a product and I think that customers won't buy it immediately, I put a sign up box that says something like "sign up for more information" and that joins them to the whole series of follow up emails, where I give them more information about the product and how it can help them.

I love this way of marketing because once it's set up, it takes care of itself and each subscriber will receive the emails in the correct order regardless of when they signed up.

I once set up a series of these emails to sell an affiliate product and I earned over $4,000 in 3 months, all on auto-pilot.

Auto-responder series do take quite bit of time to write and set up, but if done correctly, they can go on working for years.

They just need to be entertaining, informative and anticipated, and can really help with getting a product in front of prospective customers a lot more than 7 times.

And if you're promoting products through article writing, social media, email, auto responders, forums and blogs, then you should be having great success.

And that's as many ideas as I can tell you about advertising. I could say more, but I don't want you to suffer from information overload. There is also paid advertising where you pay to place ads on other websites, but that's costly so most people don't do it. And when you're first starting out, you don't want to spend too much money before you've earned some.

Just remember that everything you do online is advertising and it all starts with providing great web page content which is your best advertising of all.

Chapter 12.

How to Keep It All Going and Going

By now, if you've followed all the advice in this ebook, everything about your new laptop lifestyle should be in place.

You'll have a website online, you'll be advertising lots of products to sell, you'll have an email list of subscribers and you'll be making money advertising your own products, other people's products and any other ways you come across.

Never miss an opportunity to advertise your business or to make money.

Of course how much money you can make on a regular basis depends on your chosen niche, your website, your content and how much of everything you do or don't do.

Now I'm not saying that you should rush around grabbing everything you can and going for every money-making opportunity that you see. Not at all.

Instead I'm just saying that you should be running your own website, making some money, and seeing all the possibilities of how you can grow your business to turn it into a real financial powerhouse.

Alternatively, you can wash, rinse and repeat and start up another website in a different, or even a related niche.

Remember the guy I mentioned earlier who could only make $1/day from his website so he decided to have 50 websites just like it? That's the kind of thing I'm talking about. Not that you should have 50 $1 websites, but you should be able to see more possibilities of what else you can do once you get started.

Until you begin though, you won't be able to see what I mean. But I know it will happen, because everyone I talk to or read about online, begins with one simple website and then expands on all their ideas (all their "hell yeah!" ideas) until they have the perfect - and easy online business that they've always wanted.

And I know the same can happen for you too. You just start small and then Wham! Next thing you know you start thinking about more and more things that you want to try.

But just remember what I've been stressing to you all along though. If it doesn't appeal to you, don't do it. Don't spend the rest of your life sitting at home working on an online business that bores you.

I like writing so I write ebooks. I love ebooks because I don't need to trudge around and try and find a publisher, I don't need to worry about printing and shipping books and I can publish them with the click of my mouse (literally).

All I do is write an ebook, go over it and edit it, format it, get Buddy from CoversCorp to create a 3D cover, write my sales page, set it all up with e-Junkie or Amazon, or wherever else I'm going to sell it, do my marketing and that's it. I can then go on with writing my next ebook.

So easy. And so much fun.

I love to write. So I love what I do. It doesn't matter whether I'm writing a marketing article that I want to submit to an article directory or I'm writing an article for web page content. I'm happy no matter what it is because I love to write.

And the internet makes it all possible.

You'll also find, like I do, that once you've done something several times, you have systems in place that you can use again and again which makes things so much easier.

Once you've created a website you'll know how to create another. Once you set up an email list you can set up more. If you outsource work, once you find people that can do the work satisfactorily, you can use them again and again.

As you go along working on your new online business, you'll find businesses and other people that are perfect to help you to do exactly what you want to do.

And it all starts with that first idea. That idea where you know what you love to do and you think "If only I could make a living out of doing this..." . Well now you can because the internet and a laptop computer means you can create an online business based on just about anything.

The other day I was playing the PopCap game Zuma's Revenge. It occurred to me that playing this game is one thing that I can't create an online business around. But then again, as much as I love playing Zuma's Revenge, I wouldn't like to do it all day. Neither does thinking about playing it get me excited to wake up in the mornings or keeps me up late at night thinking about it.

It's just something I do now and again. It's not something that I'm passionate about. So it wouldn't be fun to do it for a living.

And that's what the laptop lifestyle is all about. Enjoying what you do. Your new lifestyle is something you love doing all the time.

And hopefully, by now I have shown you how to not only sit down and brainstorm what you want to do, but I hope I've also shown you how you can convert your passion into an online business that will give you the laptop lifestyle you've always dreamed of.

Start by brainstorming an idea for your website, something you love to do or are really interested in.

Write at least 6 articles/blog posts about it.

Then set up a website or blog and publish your articles.

Next, monetise your new site with PPC ads and affiliate products. Or set up a whole online store. Or sell your own products.

If you want to create your own product or write your own ebook, do it.

Or you could offer an online service if there something you can do remotely like counselling, consulting, proof reading, writing, book reviewing, tarot card readings, horoscopes, and more.

Advertise your site using Submit Express, social media, email, and any other places you can.

Then keep adding products and content and keep marketing it all.

Let your new online business grow and flourish.

So this is it now. It's time for you to start living your dream.

Don't let it stay a dream any longer. Make it your reality.

Remember, you can't change your life in a minute, but you can change direction.

So which direction are you facing? Are you facing going to work on Monday morning, every week?

Or are you facing your new work-at-home laptop lifestyle?

The choice is entirely yours.

I already have my laptop lifestyle.

How about you?

I hope to see your new business online soon.

Best Regards

Ruth Barringham

http://cheritonhousepublishing.com

Bully Me? . . . **NO MÁS! !**

Bully Me? . . . **NO MÁS! ! !**

"Bully me?
. . . no más!!!"

por Patrice Lee

Bully Me? . . . **NO MÁS! ! !**

2nd Edition, April, 2013

Título del original: *Bully Me? NO MORE!!!*
Publicado por Feinstein Development & Associates
Impreso en Los Estados Unidos de América

Edición en español: *Bully me?...no más!!!*

Library of Congress Catalog-in-Publication Data

ISBN-13: 978-0983720713
Primera edición en español: © Agosto 2012

Traducido por Ebony A. McDonald y Natividad Morillo

Ilustración de la cubierta: Bob Ivory, Jr.,
Ivory Coast Media
Diseño Interior del Contenido: Patrice Lee

Envíe toda correspondencia a: ucantbullyme@gmail.com

Este libro está dedicado al hermano más maravilloso y amoroso que una hermana podría tener. En memoria de Quincey II.

Las palabras pueden herir...mucho

"Ten cuidado con las palabras que dices,
mantenlas suaves y dulces
porque nunca se sabe de día a día
cuales tendrás que comer."

K. McCarthy

Bully Me? . . . **NO MÁS! ! !**

Contenido

Recomendación

"Bully Me? . . . NO MÁS!!" por Patrice Lee es un verdadero hallazgo. En este libro, la autora aborda el tema del acoso escolar (*bullying)*, de las causas y efectos de lo mismo y ofrece soluciones pragmáticas.

La vida, como mi familia la conocía, cambió para siempre cuando experimentamos los efectos mortales de *bullying* a través de la pérdida de nuestro amado hijo, Jared. Él sólo tenía 13 años. Mantenemos su memoria viva por un sitio web que comparte la historia de Jared.

Mi familia y yo seguimos en búsqueda de respuestas y la forma de detener el acoso escolar. Vamos a unirnos en la lucha contra el *bullying* para proteger y preservar el tesoro más valioso de la familia - nuestros hijos.

Yo recomiendo "Bully Me?...NO MÁS!!!" a los padres y a los niños porque es un problema creciente que enfrenta la juventud hoy en día. Vale mucho leerlo.

Brenda High
Madre de Jared Benjamin High
www.jaredstory.com

Prefacio

Se está acercando tu fecha de cumpleaños número 9. De hecho, solo falta dos días y hasta ahora, nunca has sido acosado en la escuela. Con tantos hablando del bullying, has comenzado a preocupar.

Pero, hoy es el día que el bully se acerca a ti. . . ¿Qué vas a hacer?

Este libro te ayudará a prepartarte para ese momento, en caso de que llegue. Bully Me?. . . No Más! fue escrito para esos niños que pueden sentirse amenazados, o se sienten temerosos de ser atacados.

Ves al bully venir, pero no hay adonde ir, ni un lugar donde esconderse. Ahora qué? No te preocupes. Bully Me?. . . No Más! ofrece consejos prácticos, y ofrece soluciones positivas que te ayudarán a mantenerte firme.

Ojalá que el bullying nunca te pase; sin embargo, ganarás conocimiento, más confianza, y puedes ayudar hacer del mundo un lugar mejor en cada vida donde el conocimiento sea compartido por medio de este libro.

Los principios básicos de la vida compartidos en este libro, si se practica diariamente, darán resultados positivos todos los días. **¡Que este libro sirva para ti y para tus seres queridos por generaciones!**

Si el contenido de este libro puede salvar la vida de un niño, siempre estaré agradecida por la vida de uno que se salvó.

Introducción

Los niños y los jóvenes pasan una tercera parte del día fuera de la casa, algunos viajando largas distancias para educarse, para estudiar con compañeros de diversos origines, culturas y costumbres. Ellos van a la escuela con una buena apariencia exterior - en sus uniformes o ropa normal, peinados, los dientes cepillados - listos para aprender.

A la mayoría de los niños se les enseña a respetar a los demás y usar los buenos modales. Pero padres, ¿Qué están haciendo con sus niños para desarrollar un buen carácter y fomentar actitudes sanas y positivas de la autoestima? ¿Sabían ustedes que hay algo que pueden hacer diariamente para fortalecer a sus hijos emocional y espiritualmente? Ustedes pueden reducir el miedo de la conducta agresiva dirigida a ellos y hacerlos a prueba de *bullying*.

Yo creo sinceramente que la mayoría de nuestros temores en la vida se encuentran en las incógnitas. En otras palabras, los padres tienen miedo de lo que no saben y los niños tienen miedo porque perciben los temores que sus padres tienen para ellos.

Los padres quieren saber que ellos han suplido las necesidades de sus niños, que han preparado completamente a sus niños para la vida, la universidad, y para cada día después. Pero en realidad

no lo saben. Así que su miedo echa raíces – en lo desconocido. En este libro, encontrarás ayuda en cada uno de estas áreas para ti y para tu hijo(a).

Sí, tú puedes ayudar a tu hijo andar con confianza en medio de los *bullies* y animarle a ofrecer apoyo a otros cuando sea necesario. Te exhorto que completes cada tarea y actividad presentada en este libro, puede ser el trampolín que necesitas para construir la autoestima y el desarrollo del niño haciéndolo más seguro.

Toma en cuenta:

Los datos estadísticos y los resultados de investigaciones que están incluidos en este libro son solamente con este fin - para informar y educar - no con la intención de inducir miedo por parte de los padres o del niño. ¿Cómo se puede tomar las medidas adecuadas o reconocer la necesidad urgente sin haber sido debidamente informado?

I.

Las estadísticas no mienten

Las estadísticas muestran que:

- Mueren un promedio de 4,400 jóvenes cada año debido al acoso escolar (*bullying).*
- El suicidio es la tercera causa principal de muerte entre nuestros jóvenes.
- La mitad de los suicidios entre los preadolescentes (de 10 a 12 años) y los adolecentes son relacionados con el *bullying*.
- Por cada suicidio entre la juventud, hay por lo menos 100 intentos de suicidio.
- Más de 14% de los estudiantes de secundaria han contemplado suicidarse.
  - 7% de los estudiantes de secundaria han intentado el suicidio.
- Según la Universidad de Yale: Una víctima del acoso es 2 a 9 veces más propensa a considerar el suicidio.
  - Las niñas de 10 a 14 años de edad pueden tener un riesgo aún mayor.

Según las noticias ABC:

- 30% de todos los estudiantes son *bullies* o víctimas de un *bully*.
- 160,000 estudiantes se quedan en casa cada día a causa del temor de ser intimidados (*bullied*).

Según el Instituto Nacional para la Seguridad y Salud Ocupacional (NIOSH)

- Existe una pérdida de empleo de hasta $19 billones y una reducción en la productividad de $3 billones debido al acoso laboral.

Estudio de caso de la Universidad de Michigan

Investigadores del Colegio de Medicina de la Universidad de Michigan estudiaron a los estudiantes de primaria en la ciudad de Ypsilanti, Michigan, que mostraron problemas de conducta como el acoso escolar. Según la profesora asistente Louise O' Brien, Ph.D., del Centro de Trastornos del Sueño de la Universidad de Michigan, "Los niños que son *bullies*, o tienen problemas de conducta en la escuela, tienen más probabilidades de estar somnolientos durante el día."

Es posible que la falta de sueño pueda llevar al *bullying* u otros comportamientos agresivos – un problema grave que muchas escuelas están enfrentando hoy en día. Los investigadores descubrieron que la somnolencia puede ser causada por varios factores, incluyendo un entorno familiar que es caótico, sueño interrumpido, o la falta de sueño debido a demasiados estímulos electrónicos de los televisores, los teléfonos celulares, o las computadoras en los dormitorios de los niños.

Este estudio enfatiza que dormir bien es tan esencial para un estilo de vida saludable como la alimentación saludable y el ejercicio. O'Brien dijo que el estudio mostró que la somnolencia es el mayor factor de los problemas de conducta.

Michigan Chronicle, Health, June 8-14, 2011.

Nota: ¿Cómo duerme tu hijo(a)? Si tu hijo es demasiado agresivo, deberías observar sus hábitos de dormir.

II.

Definiciones y características de un *bully*

Él es sólo un *bully* con disfraz

Hay una diferencia entre el niño que ha crecido en un ambiente familiar muy amoroso y el niño que nunca ha conocido o recibido el amor de madre o el amor de padre. Un niño maltratado o sin amor ve el mundo diferente, es más brusco, y habla un idioma diferente al niño que es amado.

No es como que alguien quiere ser un *bully*. Sin embargo, las circunstancias de la vida – los sueños frustrados, egos heridos, y las experiencias tempranas de una gran decepción – pueden causar que la persona se encuentre en un estado de espiral que le haga sentir desesperanzado, y esté suficientemente enojado como para hacerles daño a personas inocentes.

Aun así, no está bien intimidar o amenazar a alguien por medio de decir o hacer cosas malas contra ellos sólo porque no es feliz.

“Bully”

(Definiciones del Diccionario)

“**Bully**” – una persona que se burla, se mete con, o hiere a las personas más pequeñas o más débiles. (Traducido. The American Heritage Children’s Dictionary, Houghton Mifflin, 1986).

“**Bully**” – una persona que se burla, asusta (con conversaciones ruidosas o amenazadoras), amenaza o lastima a otros que no son tan fuertes. (Traducido. World Book Dictionary. Barnhart, 1980).

“**Bully**” – es un sustantivo que se describe como: un fanfarrón ruidoso, compañero arrogante, se distingue más por amenazas insolentes y vacías que por su valor, y dispuesto a provocar peleas; como verbo: insultar y controlar con amenazas de ruido y fanfarrón; a ser ruidoso y pendenciero. (Traducido. Noah Webster’s American Dictionary of the English Language, 1828).

Palabras relacionadas: (para tener una plena comprensión del significado de la palabra *bully*)

Insolente – estar orgulloso y altivo, con desprecio hacía los demás, dominantes con el poder, lleno de orgullo; grosero; con una arrogancia de malicia.

Amenaza – un peligro; la demostración de una determinación de causar daño a otro, la aparición

venidera de un mal o una catástrofe probable, un alborotador.

(Cita textual): Mostrar o manifestar la probabilidad de maldad o peligro en el futuro; expresar o mostrar una disposición o deseo de causar un castigo o mal a otros.

“**Principios básicos de la vida**” – Palabras de sabiduría que puede aumentar o mejorar la calidad de tu vida.

De todas maneras, ¿Quién es este *bully*?

(Una definición personal)

Un "*Bully*" es una persona, sea – hombre, mujer, niño o niña – con problemas no resueltos que le hacen tener arranques fuertes de ira hacia los demás, cuya propia angustia mental puede llevarlo a traer destrucción a los demás, a menudo afectan el estado emocional de seguridad de aquellos a los que ataca, lo cual produce emociones como el miedo, la ira o la desesperación de los demás; cuyo trauma personal o la adversidad le ha llevado a atacarlos de una manera feroz y agresiva.

La distracción de un *bully* es mantener tu mente ocupada con el miedo y la preocupación acerca de su próximo movimiento en tu contra. Él (ella) está en una misión para evitar el logro de tu propósito en la vida.

"*Bullies*" atacan, de forma inesperada desde el principio, sin ninguna razón aparente. Parecen ser muy miserables o infelices, y parece que nunca han tenido un buen día.

Muchos *bullies* tienen malos recuerdos de una infancia infeliz, y podrían guardar rencor contra alguien que les ha causado angustia emocional por varios meses, incluso años. Estas personas, en particular, son aquellos que nunca recibieron amor de sus padres, y en su lugar experimentaron el rechazo.

Lo que desean es el verdadero amor y la aceptación, pero sus emociones pueden ser suprimidas por el dolor.

La ausencia de amor de parte de sus padres durante la infancia puede ser un factor en su comportamiento agresivo. Él (ella) puede haber sido traumatizado por algún tipo de abuso o al experimentar decepciones, como miedo, dolor, y tristeza. Estos problemas no resueltos pueden convertirse en ira.

Al igual que un niño muestra enojo haciendo una rabieta, el "*bully*" expresa su ira a través de sus acciones en contra de los demás. Por lo general, alguien que aparenta ser más débil que él. En pocas palabras, el *bully* es un cobarde.

Características de un verdadero bully

Sabrás que estás en presencia de un "*bully*" si él es:

- muy malo o despreciable.
- te hace sentir pequeño.
- tiene arranques inesperados o al azar.
- hace declaraciones exageradas acerca de ti.
- te avergüenza delante de los demás.
- hace acusaciones falsas con el intento de dañar.
- totalmente negativo hacia ti la mayoría de las veces, si no todo el tiempo.
- actúa a menudo en presencia de los demás;
- generalmente ama una audiencia.

Su objetivo es:

- disminuir totalmente tu autoestima porque el no tiene.
- aplastar tu ego mientras que el desarrolla el suyo.
- provocar miedo en ti para esconder los suyos.
- intencionalmente busca hacerte daño emocional porque él está sufriendo.
- avergonzarte porque no tiene conciencia.
- hacerte parecer débil, y él hacerse fuerte, con el fin de distraerte o desanimarte con

preocupaciones acerca de su próximo movimiento.

. . . y su efecto (s) en la víctima

- parece ser más grande que la vida misma
- se siente como que nunca va a terminar
- volverte miedoso/temeroso
- desarrollar una baja autoestima,
- desarrollar sentimientos de impotencia, desesperanza o desesperación.
- desarrollar niveles más profundos de miedo, mientras el acoso continúa.
- llegar a ser totalmente abrumado si continúa por mucho tiempo.

"Bully" clasificado

Hay muchos tipos de *bullies*. En este libro, vamos a destacar los más reconocidos por sus delitos. Vamos a empezar con el "*Bully del Aula*".

El "Bully del Aula"

El *bully* del salón de clases es uno de los cuales estamos familiarizados. El típico *bully* de la clase era el niño que molestaba a las niñas y a los niños en el aula y después de la escuela. Este *bully* ha sido conocido por burlarse/tomar el pelo, empujar, tomar bolígrafos, lápices y otros útiles de un estudiante y ocultarlos o ponerlos en una mochila de otro estudiante. Estos útiles no siempre eran recuperados.

La mayoría de las veces, el *bully* del salón de clases es lo suficientemente inteligente como para no ser atrapado, y por lo general, elige hacer su movimiento cuando su compañero es más vulnerable – que es – cuando el maestro está fuera del aula. El *bully* de clase clásico nunca ha sido específico de género.

Un cambio de asiento puede ser la solución inmediata, si las bromas se inician en el aula. La mejor defensa es pedir en secreto al profesor un cambio de asiento, que esté tan lejos de él/ella como sea posible, esperando que el cambio de asiento traiga la solución total del problema.

Hoy en día, los *bullies* son más específicos en el género. Los niños tienden a elegir a los niños, y las

niñas, en el salón de clases, tienden a dirigir más su atención hacia otras niñas.

Los niños y niñas, hombres y mujeres jóvenes, deben tener cuidado en los baños, pasillos y corredores traseros de las escuelas, edificios y áreas desconocidas. La mayoría de los pasillos de las escuelas, baños, escaleras, y las cafeterías son monitoreados constantemente para la seguridad de los niños.

Un estudiante en la escuela intermedia o secundaria puede recibir más ataques verbales o físicos de un *bully* en el tiempo de recreo, durante la práctica deportiva, o después de la escuela. En estos lugares es donde los niños pueden llegar a ser más rudos de lo que serían dentro de un salón de clases, sobre todo cuando el profesor no esta presente.

Todo tipo de acoso escolar deber ser reportado a las autoridades correspondientes. Cuanto antes, mejor. Tus padres y tus profesores deben ser informados, así la situación puede estar bajo control. Si el acoso se inicia en el aula, puede continuar fuera del aula, si no se controla de inmediato

El "Bully de Recreo"

Este "*bully*" probablemente no es el mejor deportista; por lo tanto, quiere asegurarse de que nadie más lo haga bien en los deportes. Esta es un área donde realmente pueden ser agresivos, sobre todo con los chicos. Aunque las niñas han empezado a ser más agresivas también.

A veces se burlan y llaman a otro de sus compañeros del equipo con sobrenombres. Después de que el sobrenombre ha sido bien recibido por los demás, el *bully* continua con violencia física ya sea empujando o tirando pelotas (u otros objetos) a su victima, mientras que constantemente busca el apoyo de sus compañeros.

La reacción de sus compañeros – su apoyo, o la falta de – pueden desempeñar un papel importante aquí. Si los demás miembros del equipo defienden a la víctima del *bully*, este escenario puede convertirse en un ambiente positivo.

Sin embargo, si no esta bajo control, alguien puede salir lastimado gravemente. Es mejor para todo el mundo mostrar su apoyo colectivo a favor de la victima e informar a las autoridades correspondientes. El ser honesto puede ayudar a prevenir la muerte o heridas graves.

"El Bully del barrio"

Los *bullies* del barrio no son necesariamente de la zona de su residencia, pero podría ser alguien que elige selectivamente a alguien en su área, por razones conocidas o desconocidas. Esta es una área donde los padres y los buenos vecinos deben trabajar juntos a través de asociaciones de vecinos, carros de seguridad privada y otros métodos de vigilancia para mantener las áreas donde viven seguras.

"El Bully del internet"

Creciendo en popularidad es el "*bully del internet*". Este monstruo acosador, debajo de la apariencia de los medios sociales, está haciendo mucho daño. Las estadísticas muestran que las niñas son las más afectadas.

La presión de grupo, especialmente entre las relaciones de los niños y niñas, el círculo de chicas, etc., han demostrado ser muy perjudiciales. Este "bully" toma todas las cosas malas que normalmente diría en frente de un grupo pequeño o en el aula y las comparte en el espacio cibernético, para que todo el mundo (World Wide Web) pueda verlo. Esto penetra en su espíritu aún más cuando está en forma escrita, porque sabe que tiene posibilidades infinitas.

Sólo unas pocas palabras negativas sobre una discusión de un tema delicado o un falso testimonio, puede aplastar los sueños, estropear el amor propio, bajar la autoestima, y destruir la reputación de uno.

El efecto devastador es que uno no sabe cuánto tiempo estas palabras destructivas circularan antes de que la situación se calme. Uno sólo puede imaginar la amenaza continua y perpetua de las circunstancias y las consecuencias debilitantes.

Niños, es importante tener reglas para supervisar y controlar la actividad en la computadora. Confía en tus padres o en un adulto responsable que te guiará en esta área, ya que esto ayudará a preservar y proteger tu futuro.

Tú tienes un propósito para estar en esta tierra, y no es pasar tres o cuatro horas al día molestando gente en el internet. Tus talentos no pueden ser nutridos y desarrollados cuando no haces nada productivo.

No me malinterprete, Facebook® y Twitter® tienen un propósito, que consiste en aumentar y mejorar las comunicaciones en todo el mundo. Sin embargo, fue con el intento para hacerse de una manera positiva, para obtener resultados positivos.

El acoso cibernético se ha convertido en una de las formas más letales de ataque, tan devastadoras en niños y adolescentes, que es el medio que trae más resultados fatales.

Tu tarea #1: Pide prestado el DVD del Mago de Oz de tu biblioteca pública y estudia los patrones en el comportamiento del león. Llevarás la ventaja sobre el *bully* la próxima vez que se acerque. **:)**

III.

Confianza en uno mismo

¿No puedes ver lo que tú me has hecho?

Bully, ¿No puedes ver lo que tú me has hecho?

Estaba asustado y tímido.
Tú me hiciste sentir inseguro.
Me impactó emocionalmente. Me convertí en una persona reservada.

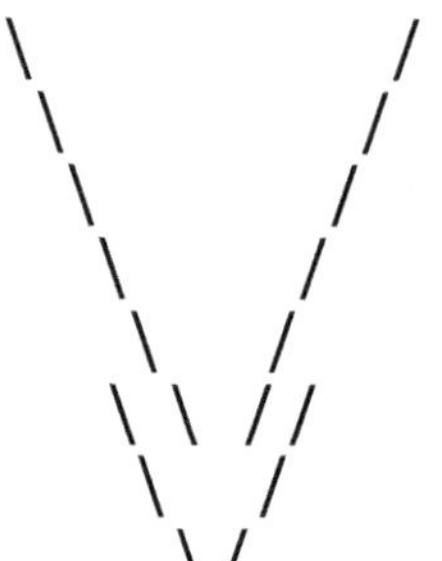

Entonces decidí no dejarte estar cerca de mí.
Decidí perseverar y
¡Ser fuerte!

Sé fuerte

Vamos a hablar por un momento acerca de las cosas que haces bien, con poco esfuerzo. Esas son tus fortalezas. Es importante que tú conozcas tus fortalezas porque durante esos momentos cuando eres más vulnerable – en la presencia de un *bully*- es cuando tus debilidades parecerán más grandes.

¿Cuales son tus fortalezas? Menciona dos de ellas. Enfócate en esas fortalezas, y algunas nuevas que descubras.

Es importante que tú seas fuerte, pero cuando se trata de ser *bullied*, no puedes hacerlo sólo. Todos necesitan a alguien en quien apoyarse de vez en cuando.

Niños, tus padres quieren escuchar de ti. Por favor, mantén la puerta de la comunicación abierta entre ustedes, así podrás hablar de cualquier cosa.

El hogar es el mejor lugar para hablar, dar un abrazo, reír o tener un buen llanto. Llorar libera el cuerpo del estrés. Te vas a sentir mejor después de haber llorado.

¿No sabías que Dios nunca está muy ocupado y que Él nunca falla? Él es el único de quien puedes apoyarte y confiar todo el tiempo, no importa qué.

Él estará ahí para ti cuando nadie más esté disponible. Tú puedes confiar que Él puede trabajar en cualquier problema o situación. Puedes depender de Su fuerza.
¿Sabes lo que Dios dice? "La venganza es mía, yo pagaré". Esto simplemente significa que Él se encargará de cualquiera que decida hacer lo malo, y

cualquiera que venga en contra tuya. Tu trabajo es orar por ellos y perdonar sus ofensas en tu contra.

¡Necesitas saber que **eres un Ganador**!

Si tú has sido atacado por un "bully", primero déjame decirte que tú eres un ganador. ¿Cómo lo sé? Bueno, tú obviamente tienes algo que el bully quiere. Quizás, él ha visto cuan feliz tú eres; o quizás tú tienes muchos amigos, familia y personas que realmente cuidan de tu bienestar. Quizás tú has tenido buenas notas en la escuela y los profesores te aman.

Tal vez tú eres bendecido con cosas materiales. O, podría ser que tú tienes algo que él quiere. Quizás tú eres talentoso y haces las cosas bien en tu equipo deportivo. Tal vez tú eres uno de esos chicos lindos o una hermosa jovencita que es admirada por tus compañeros. ¿Quién sabe lo que hay en la mente de un bully? Él usualmente no hace nada por razonamiento a sus rivales. Él los ataca sin ninguna razón.

No dejes que la conducta del bully te cambie. Continua siendo la persona maravillosa que eres. Sin embargo, tú debes actuar o reaccionar con rapidez si él te ataca para que las cosas no se salgan de control. Lo que quiero decir es que tú nunca debes dejar que tus emociones sean alteradas. Y nunca dejar al bully tomar lo mejor de ti. Aun cuando pienses que lo tiene, no dejes que él lo sepa.

Confía en que Dios se encargará de tu situación con el bully como sólo Él puede hacerlo. Las promesas de Dios para nosotros en Su Palabra es que Él peleará nuestras batallas. Él es el único que puede pelear con el bully y ganar. De hecho Él siempre gana.

Así que deja que Él maneje esto por ti. Con Él a tu lado, también eres un ganador. Así es cómo El muestra su poder.

Arréglate

Ya hemos hablado suficiente de los bullies y lo que hacen. Ahora, nos enfocaremos en soluciones de cómo arreglar el quebranto que ha causado e incorporar remedios para las emociones que han sido heridas por los efectos del bully.

Si has sido confrontado por un bully, este es el momento para verte mejor porque cuanto mejor te veas, mejor te sentirás. Y mientras mejor te sientas, más derrotado el enemigo – el bully – se sentirá.

¿Tienes ropa en el closet que nunca te has puesto? ¿Tienes un par de medias, una camisa o blusa, un conjunto o suéter que tú has guardado para una ocasión especial?

Bueno, ¡Este es tu día especial! ¡Sácalos del closet, y póntelos!:)

Cuando te pones tus mejores medias o suéter- o cualquier cosa que decidas usar- úsalo con una sonrisa, y úsalo todo el día. Celebra la vida. Hoy el mundo está celebrando la vida contigo.

Después que estés completamente vestido, mira al

espejo, date a ti mismo un gran abrazo y di ¨Te amo (di tu nombre)¨ y también di, ¨¡Hoy va hacer un gran día!¨

Usa tu ropa favorita – estilos y colores – la forma en que te sientas bien contigo mismo. Levántate. Mantén una sonrisa en tu rostro.
De hecho, no ha terminado hasta que – los mirones, los negativos, y por supuesto, el bully - vean que tú has ganado. Cuando tú luces y te sientes bien, tú puedes ser mejor tanto por dentro como por fuera. Esa es la idea, verse y sentirse victorioso hasta que veas tu victoria. Yeah!!

También, esta actividad ha sido tomada de la sección "Las características de un verdadero bully", la cual se encuentra a final del libro:

Aquí hay una actividad que puedes hacer con tu familia.

Mira estos programas en la TV:

Vamos a llamarlo ¨Encuentra el bully ahora¨. El objetivo es encontrar el bully de las siguientes caricaturas. Después discute las acciones del bully con tus padres.

Lista de Caricaturas:

Bugs Bunny

Popeye

El corre camino

El gato Silvestre y Piolín

====➔===➔

> > “Avanzando. . . ” > >

Superando esos sentimientos de rechazo

"Palos y Piedras pueden romper mis huesos, pero las palabras nunca me herirán" Esto no es cierto.

Cuando tú has sido herido o rechazado por las personas que tú amas y cuidas, la mejor cosa que tú puedes hacer es perdonarlos. Lo más pronto que tú perdones, lo más rápido serás sanado y menos será la posibilidad de que muestres enojo, hostilidad, u otras emociones negativas.

La misma regla se aplica a ellos que han sido maltratados, burlados o *bullied* por sus compañeros. Si alguien te ha herido, avergonzado o humillado de alguna forma, la cosa más importante que puedes hacer—después de reportarlo--es perdonarlos. Esto no es tan fácil como suena. Al principio no es una idea que te hace sentir bien. Sin embargo, una vez que el perdón se activa, mejor te sentirás, más saludable serás, y mucho más fuerte serás.

Perdonar al instante, te ayudará a mantener un carácter mas agradable durante todo el día, el objetivo es que cada día sea un día tranquilo y feliz.

Otra manera de superar el rechazo es revertirlo. En otras palabras, buscando la parte chistosa en lo que el *bully* dice acerca de ti y reír de sus comentarios. No sólo lo atraparás fuera de base, eso lo dejará confundido, intrigado, pasmado. Él se marchará derrotado. ¡Si! ¡Ganaste!

Siempre debes saber que no importa cuál sea el resultado, Dios te ama, y Él cuida de todos tus problemas. El amor de Dios es incondicional.

IV.

Todo va a estar bien

Un Cambio

Oye *Bully*, hoy oré por ti.
Cuando hablé con Dios, no sabía que decirle.
Tus palabras, tus risas eran tan feroces y fuertes.
"Dios", le dije, "Esto ya ha durado demasiado tiempo."

Oye *Bully*, estoy orando por ti.
¿Qué otra opción tengo yo?
Tus palabras me lastiman y me dan tristeza.
Me hiciste ver que Dios es mi único amigo.

Cuando oré, ¿Sabes lo que dije yo?
"Ya no aguanto más, prefiero estar . . ."
Cuando pensé en estas palabras que grité,
Le pedí perdón a Dios, y en seguida, a ti **te perdoné**.

Oye *Bully,* ahora cuando oro
Le voy a pedir a Dios que yo sea un amigo para ti.
Si lo permites, él hará todas las cosas nuevas.
Porque tú también un cambio necesitarás.

Ahora cuando te veo,
Te miro a través de los ojos del amor.
Veo a una persona sedienta del amor verdadero,
Y no el *bully* que antes me molestaba.

Que Dios te dé la paz, como me la ha dado a mí.
Él es el Único que te puede salvar y liberar
De los pensamientos que te atormentan
Y llenarte con su amor, el verdadero amor – incondicional.

Gigante formidable

Había un tiempo cuando te parecías un gigante
formidable.
Tan lleno de odio y conflictos.

Por alguna razón, no podía entender
Cómo te enfocabas en mí el día entero.

Simplemente, elegí vivir la vida feliz.
Y yo era feliz, sólo por ser yo

Fue mi decisión de no hacerte caso
En cambio, levanté la cabeza en fe y creí

Que Dios no me dejaría
Porque sabía que me cuidaba.

Simplemente, elegí vivir la vida feliz.
Yo era feliz, sólo por ser yo.

¡Oye *bully*!

Oye *bully*,

Me ayudaba crecer,
Porque ahora yo sé.
No fue culpa mía
Que me molestaras.

Pero en la oscuridad
De tu mirada feroz
Yo no podría ver
Dónde esta experiencia me iba a llevar.

Ahora, soy un sobreviviente.
Tú ves
Sólo estabas ayudándome.

Yo tenía que crecer
Para ayudar a mi prójimo
En solidaridad
Nos levantamos firmes y fuertes.

¡Sí, tú puedes!

Yo tenía que experimentar esto
Para ayudarte a ti...
En el caso de que seas una víctima también.

Sólo quiero que sepas . . . .
<u>¡Tú puedes hacerlo!</u>

V.

Estás en zona segura

Eligiendo un sistema de apoyo

(Si tú has sido atacado)

Ser atacado por un *bully* es agotador. Y si tú has sido atacado más de una vez, podrías sentirte impotente y podrías estar buscando respuestas. Yo te digo: "¡*Felicidades*!, porque sobreviviste. Y si estás leyendo este libro, ya estás en camino hacía tu recuperación."

Todos necesitan ayuda en alguna etapa de su vida y definitivamente, esto es uno de esos momentos. Por favor no estés demasiado avergonzado para pedir ayuda.

Si eres niño, adolescente, joven, o un adulto bajo ataque, tú necesitas un sistema de apoyo que ayuda a mantenerte fuerte. Si ya te sientes derrotado, necesitas este tipo de soporte para recuperarte nuevamente.

Aquí es donde varias victimas se equivocan. Ellos esperan hasta que son tan maltratados por el enemigo—o el *bully* en este caso—que le queda muy poca o nada de fuerza. No trate de hacer esto solo. Inmediatamente después de ser atacado por un *bully*, busca un sistema de apoyo. Si eliges el sistema de apoyo correcto, te mantendrá fuerte, y detendrá al *bully* también.

Algunas Sugerencias:

1. Dios. El Todopoderoso. (Disponible 24 horas al día)
2. Estar cerca de la familia—madre, padre, abuela, abuelo, etc.
3. Estar cerca de los amigos-alguien que tú confías.

4. Consejeros profesionales- busca ayuda profesional de tu pastor, consejero escolar, o consejeros privados en una agencia de consejería local.
5. Director de la escuela, profesores, consejeros.
6. Todo lo anterior.

Además de estas sugerencias, podrías considerar la creación de un “sistema de bully” o “red” de amigos que estarán dispuestos a apoyarte. Este “sistema de bully” se aseguraría de que nunca estarías solo y juntos, tú y tus compañeros pueden apoyarse y protegerse mutuamente. Hay fuerza en los números.

Bully me? ? ? ? . . .

El acto de una persona intimidando (*bullying)* a otra persona es una batalla que afecta la victima emocionalmente y psicológicamente. Puede ser que tu interacción con él no te afecta físicamente pero sí puede afectar tu espíritu.

Para las chicas, el acto de *bullying* es sobre todo psicológico. No se me mal interprete. Esta lucha te afecta tanto como un encuentro físico porque todo lo que hacemos o que estamos tratando de llegar a ser, comienza en la mente.

Los chicos, generalmente, comienza con un ataque mental y luego avanzan a un ataque físico a medida que progresa la intimidación (*bullying).* En cuanto más progresa el *bullying*, más físico podría llegar a ser.

No se recomienda que pelee, pero es imprescindible que corras a buscar ayuda. Sencillamente niégate a involucrarse físicamente.

Tú puedes, además, usar las armas espirituales de Dios para pelear las batallas contra el enemigo. Ellas son más poderosas que cualquier fuerza negativa operando a través de una sola persona.

Deja que Dios transforme tus pensamientos con Su Palabra. Permite que Él renueve tu mente y refresque

tus pensamientos. Libérate de ser la **victima** a través de Su palabra.

Porque Dios no te ha dado un espíritu de cobardía, sino de poder, amor, y una mente sana. De modo que mientras caminas en Su amor, Él te dará una nueva confianza y una nueva actitud hacia la vida.

Poniéndote la armadura...

(Vestirse para la batalla)

Ahora que hemos establecido el hecho de que esta batalla es sobre todo espiritual, tienes que estar preparado para la batalla. ¿Puedo presentarte la forma en que debes estar vestido para dicha ocasión?

Debes ponerte tu armadura fielmente al igual que te vistes todos los días para ir a la escuela o al trabajo. Tu armadura debe ser puesta antes de tu vestimenta física. (Tendrás que usar la imaginación, por supuesto). Tal vez hayas adivinado que te estás poniendo un equipo de protección para mantener tus emociones bajo control. Y si tomas el tiempo para hacer los pasos a continuación, harás una diferencia en tu día.

Como ya hemos establecido que esta no es una batalla de carne y hueso, esto es lo que debes hacer:

1. *"Ciñe tus lomos con la verdad"*. Decide hablar palabras de verdad hoy mismo.

2. "*Vístete con la coraza de justicia*". Mantén un corazón puro. Camina en buenos términos con Dios.

3. *"Calza tus pies con la preparación del evangelio de la paz"*. Deja que la paz comience y termine contigo. Mantén la calma. Todo estará bien.

4. "Toma el escudo de la fe para apagar los dardos de fuego" que tu enemigo (el *bully*) te apunta, por ejemplo, las falsas acusaciones, malas palabras o acciones, y hacerte el blanco de sus bromas. Sólo cree lo mejor de ti. Entiende que Dios te ama. "...

*porque está escrito, mía es la venganza; yo pagaré, dice el Señor". (*Romanos 12:19).

5. "*Coloca el yelmo de salvación en tu cabeza"*. Da tu corazón a Jesús. Él te mantendrá a salvo. Recíbelo a Él como Señor de tu vida.

6. *"Toma la espada del espíritu, que es la palabra de Dios"*, y aplícala en tu vida diariamente. (Tomado de Efesios 6:10-18). Hay un versículo de la Biblia para cada problema y reto que enfrentas. Para todos los aficionados a la tecnología, hay una "app" en la Biblia para todo lo que necesitas. Sólo haz clic (búscala) y descarga la Palabra de Dios en tu corazón. Y piensa en ella día y noche.

7. *"Ora siempre"*. Habla con Dios. Él es real; solo no puedes verlo. Él está disponible para ti y quiere oír de ti. Él pone mucha atención a los detalles. Él se preocupa mucho por ti. Habla las promesas de Dios de su Palabra cuando ores y recuérdale de ellas. Si tienes un problema con el miedo, puedes hablar con Él de esta manera: "**Padre Celestial, Tu Palabra dice que** "*no me has dado espíritu de cobardía, sino de poder, de amor y de dominio propio*" (2 Timoteo 1:7) Por lo tanto, no voy a tener miedo.

Al hacer estos siete pasos, mantente firme en lo que crees. Entiende que Dios está trabajando para ti. Y observa cómo se realiza.

Cuando tienes esta armadura puesta, estás rodeado por la presencia de Dios. Una vez que estés completamente vestido, toma un paso atrás y deja que Dios haga el resto. ☺ Es así de fácil.

Es imposible que alguien penetre la presencia de Dios que está a tu alrededor. Tú estás cubierto, protegido y a salvo, y en Su *"presencia hay plenitud de gozo"* (Salmo 16:11). *Este es el secreto para ganar la batalla en todo momento.*

Sugerencia: Confía en Dios. Entre menos te quejes de tus problemas, más pronto van a terminar. (¿Has leído sobre el viaje de los israelitas que duraron 40 años en el desierto, lo cual debería haber tomado sólo 11 días? Se encuentra en el libro de Éxodo. Mira lo que pasó en su viaje... porque eligieron murmurar y quejarse.)

Tus brazos son demasiados cortos para pelear con Dios

Bully, ¿No puedes ver?
Tus brazos son demasiados cortos para pelear con Dios.
Voy a sentarme y tomar todo con calma,
Porque eso es lo que se hace cuando Dios está de tu lado.

Bully, ¿No puedes ver?
Tus brazos son demasiados cortos para pelear con Dios y yo.
La vida es sólo una batalla perdida con un precio muy alto,
Hasta que nos damos cuenta de lo que somos en Cristo.

Ahora, ¿No puedes ver que
Tus brazos son demasiados cortos para pelear con Dios y yo?
Sin Él no tendrás descanso,
No hay paz, ni alegría, ni felicidad.

Oh bully, tienes que ver que
Tus brazos son demasiados cortos para pelear con Dios y yo.

Sé que puedo hacer todas las cosas por medio de Cristo

Que me fortalece, incluso si esto significa

Ignorar las cosas terribles que tú haces.

Oye Bully, sólo quiero que sepas que estaré orando por ti.

Pero yo os digo: "*Amad a vuestros enemigos, bendecid a los que os maldicen, haced bien a los que os aborrecen, y orad por los que os ultrajan y os persiguen*".
(Mateo 5:44).

VI.

Defendiéndote

No es tu culpa que Él es un b*ully*

Ya es tiempo que el *Bully* tome responsabilidad por
los problemas que ha causado.
Porque va a seguir si no se detiene.
Su forma de echarte la culpa es en vano,
El *bully* culpa a la víctima, aun cuando la culpa no le
pertenece.

Considera orar por él, y trata de ser amable.
Él está perturbado con emociones desagradables.
No queriendo hacer daño, Él sólo necesita ser amado;
Y saber que está cuidado por el Padre en el cielo.

(Si el *bully* hubiera sabido esto, él no te hubiera
molestado).

“Esquiva la pelota”
“El juego que sigue durante toda la vida.”

El Quemado (también conocido como El Balón Prisionero o El Matado) era un juego que jugábamos durante la clase de deportes o durante el recreo en la escuela primaria. Para mí, fue el juego más divertido entre todos. La idea del juego es esquivar la pelota cada vez que es lanzada. Estaría fuera del juego si fuera golpeado por la pelota.

El juego de El Quemado fue divertido no importa si fuera la persona lanzando la pelota o si fuera la persona esquivándola con éxito cada vez que fue lanzada. Había un gran sentido de logro y de orgullo por haber estado en el juego hasta el final.

Ahora, vamos a transferir la idea de este juego de El Quemado a la mente. De este modo, tu reacción no será física, sino mental. Miraremos cómo podemos prepararnos para ganar sin ningún tipo de cicatrices de guerra.

En el juego de esquivar la pelota, no tienes que ser bueno en los deportes. Pero este juego mental sí exige una verdadera necesidad de fortalecer tus músculos espirituales. Necesitarás usar tu fuerza interior y tu capacidad de perdonar, como parte de tu método de operación. También tendrás que practicar el autocontrol.

Esto puede obligarte estirar tu fe.

Comienza con la paciencia, el pensamiento positivo, un apetito saludable por lo bueno, integridad, y un corazón lleno de amor. . . . Puede ser doloroso al

principio. Sin embargo, la práctica de este ejercicio espiritual regularmente te ayudará a prepararte para las pelotas que se presentarán.

Vamos a examinar algunos de los pasos implicados.

1. Pon a Dios primero. Reconoce a Dios cada mañana y pídele su guía y protección.
2. Mantén una actitud positiva y una sonrisa durante el día.
3. Nunca respondas de forma negativa a una persona que está en tu contra. Finge como si no lo oyeras.
4. Perdona, aun cuando te duela. Y suelta el dolor tan pronto como perdones.
5. Reporta las amenazas de un *bully* de inmediato a una persona de autoridad. (Debe ser una persona que tiene tu confianza y el mejor interés de corazón).

Ahora tú estás listo(a) para la pelota cuando se presente. Estás defendiéndote cada vez que decides esquivar la pelota.

Nota: Mientras que tú estás perfeccionando tu método de operación contra el territorio del enemigo, Dios está peleando en tu nombre.

***Bullies* Adultos** (más allá del salón de clase)

Los adultos pueden ser *bullied*; y los adultos pueden ser *bullies* también.

Como los adultos están leyendo este libro también, dedicaremos las próximas páginas sobre el tema para ellos. Puede ser que hayas observado o experimentado los siguientes comportamientos de los adultos.

El acoso puede seguir fuera de la escuela y el aula. Si no se aborda el problema desde el principio, puede continuar hasta la adultez y en el lugar de trabajo. A veces el *bully* podría ser tu jefe. ☹ Por falta de mejor término, los llamaremos "Los Jefes Acosadores".

Si un *bully adulto* está en una posición de autoridad sobre ti, el podría usar esa autoridad como un arma de destrucción masiva. En otros términos, el "Jefe Acosador", por ser jefe, podría gritarte insultos o asignarte cargas excesivas como una extensión de su ira.

Es razonable pensar que los niños con problemas no resueltos de abuso verbal o de otra forma guarden sentimientos de inseguridad, enojo, infelicidad, envidia, etc., hasta la adultez. Estas emociones negativas de su niñez, cuando son desenmascaradas, tienden a magnificarse en el adulto, causando mucho trauma emocional a las personas que se encuentren en su camino.

Mientras que el acoso escolar de un niño es un asunto muy serio y ha tenido resultados fatales, una víctima adulta del acoso laboral puede tener graves repercusiones. Además, el sustento de la persona

adulta podría ser afectado debido a la pérdida de salario, cambio de puesto, etc.

Si tú estás experimentando el acoso laboral, es posible que trabajes para un jefe infeliz y afligido emocionalmente. Puede ser que necesites emplear algunas de las mismas estrategias que aprendiste en la escuela primaria (de cómo esquivar la pelota) como en el juego "El Quemado".

Entonces, cuando te encuentres con ese "jefe acosador", y sabes que eres el blanco, esquiva la pelota. (El jefe es la pelota; tú eres el blanco.) ☺ Y si el "jefe acosador" habla mentiras sobre ti o te acusa falsamente, tú puedes esquivar la pelota siguiendo los pasos de las páginas anteriores.

Mientras que haces esos 5 pasos, no te olvides de:

1. Proteger tus pensamientos cuidadosamente. Refrescarlos constantemente con palabras e ideas positivas.

2. Pregúntate a ti mismo, ¿Qué puedo hacer hoy para hacer a alguien feliz?

A medida que practicas estos dos pasos, estás construyendo el carácter y ganarás al mismo tiempo. **¡A Ganar!** Esquivar la pelota tiene muchas recompensas. Más, se siente bien ganar. ☺

<u>Nota Especial</u>:
Cuando hayas llegado al punto más difícil o más incómodo es cuando tu victoria está lo más cerca.

Nota a los niños: ¿Están sorprendidos que los *bullies* continúen su misión hasta la edad adulta si no se detienen desde el principio? Por esta razón, debes reaccionar rápidamente cuando estás acosado (*bullied*). Buscar apoyo no significa que eres débil, ni que eres un fracasado. El *bully* necesita ayuda, y tú puedes tener un papel importante al ayudarlo a que la consiga.

Negarte a ser encajonado

(Vive fuera de la caja)

Las fuerzas negativas – el *bully* incluido - trabajan para mantenerte encajonado en el mismo lugar año tras año. El trabajo del enemigo es mantenernos dónde estamos, para contenernos. Pero hay que resistir las fuerzas de contención.

Dios quiere que tú continúes creciendo y ser la mejor persona que puedas. Cuando experimentes dificultades, recuerda que sólo es una prueba. No permitas que las heridas del pasado y las decepciones te roben tus sueños.

Mantén una buena actitud a pesar de los tiempos difíciles, y verás que las puertas comenzarán a abrirse para ti. Experimentarás crecimiento, y con crecimiento te moverás a una dimensión de oportunidades infinitas. Allí es dónde tus sueños se realizarán.

VII.

Enfócate en tus sueños

Siempre haz lo mejor, sé lo mejor, y espera lo mejor.

O

Ñ

E

U

"S **EN GRANDE"**

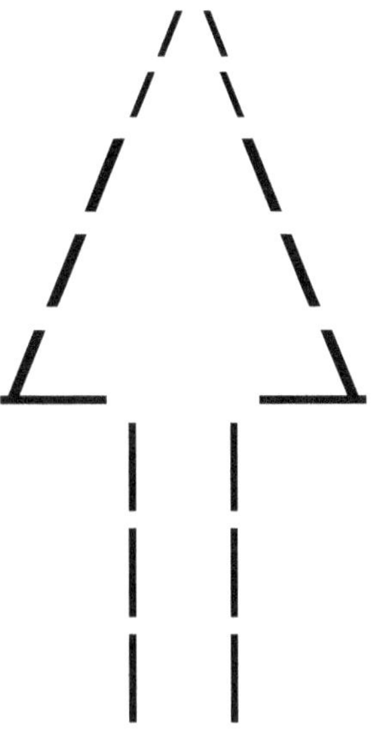

\- -el cielo es el límite- - /

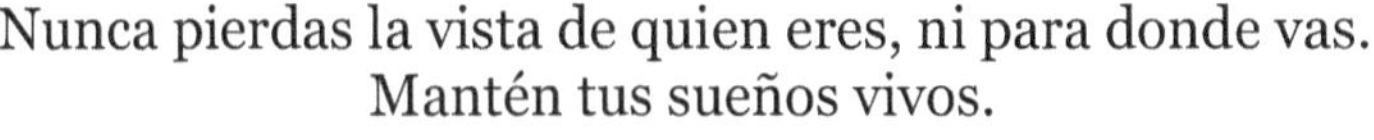

Nunca pierdas la vista de quien eres, ni para donde vas.
Mantén tus sueños vivos.

Saliendo para tener éxito

(Más allá del ataque)

Aquí hay algunas cosas que tú puedes hacer para acelerar el proceso de sanación.

1. Mantén una buena actitud. Refresca tu mente constantemente con afirmaciones y pensamientos positivos.
2. Ora. Pide a Dios por Sus bendiciones para tu vida.
3. Vive cada día con gran expectativa que buenas cosas te pasarán.
4. Evita las distracciones. No pienses en las heridas pasadas y las decepciones. Ignora las palabras negativas.
5. Enfócate en tus objetivos, sueños y aspiraciones.
6. Vive cada día para el mañana, pero disfruta cada momento de cada día.

Para dar un resume:

Conoce que el cambio ya viene. Dile a Dios lo que tú quieres y cree que lo recibirás. Vive con gran expectativa cada día.

Como recibes las bendiciones de Dios y las respuestas a tus oraciones, confía que Él trabajará en los detalles. Tú tienes un futuro maravilloso por delante. Así que sueña, establece metas, anótalas, planifica y sueña un poco más. El cielo es el límite.

Orar

Perdonar **Soñar**

Amor

Mirando a través de los ojos del amor.

Orar

Dios siempre está disponible cuando tú lo llamas. De hecho, Él ama escuchar de ti. Él es el Único quien puede cambiar el corazón de una persona malintencionada. La oración es una de las claves para el futuro.

Perdón

El perdón es de suma importancia. Debes perdonar para que 1) puedas ser perdonado, 2) tus oraciones sean contestadas, y 3) para que puedas ser sanado emocionalmente. Después de todo, Dios dijo: "Mía es la venganza, Yo pagaré." Esto significa que Él se encargará de cualquier persona que opta por hacerte daño.

Sueño

Cuando ores, perdona. Cuando tú perdonas, caminas en amor. Esto libera tu espíritu para soñar. Tu mente está limpia para pensar en buenas cosas, y tu cuerpo no lleva cargas día tras día.

Amor

Este es el gran mandamiento para todos. Amor es la fuerza motriz que nos impulsa a perdonar. ". . . *pero el mayor de ellos es el amor*" (1 Corintios 13:13).

Cuerpo, alma y espíritu están conectados. Tú limpias tu mente cuando perdonas. Tú liberas tu espíritu cuando hablas con Dios a través de la oración; y te sientes absolutamente genial cuando agregas el amor a tu rutina diaria.

Practica mirando a través de los ojos del amor con cada persona que te encuentres. . .

VIII.

Aprendiendo amar a los desagradables

Niños: Ustedes son amados

Dios te ama mucho y su amor es incondicional. Él te ama aun cuando eres desagradable.

- Él te ama aun cuando le faltes el respeto al hablarle a tus padres y maestros, aunque no deberías hablarles así.
- Él te ama todavía, aun cuando no dices la verdad, cuando no compartes con los demás, o cuando actúas como que hiciste tus tareas, pero no las hiciste.
- Él todavía te ama cuando dices que no comiste la última galleta, pero sí lo hiciste.
- Y Él todavía te ama cuando eres desobediente. Sólo recuerda que hay consecuencias que tendrás que pagar.

El amor de Dios es maravilloso; es un amor eterno. Sométete a Él para que puedas cosechar todos sus beneficios. Una vez que te das cuenta de la profundidad de su amor, entonces puedes amar a los demás a través de su ejemplo.

Él te ha proporcionado de todas las herramientas necesarias para tener una vida exitosa. Encontrarás estas herramientas en la Biblia. Puedes acceder a ellas y aplicarlas en cada área de tu vida.

Al estudiar La Palabra, encontrarás escrituras que se aplican al área específica de tu necesidad. Si necesitas

ayuda, Dios está dispuesto para ayudarte. Si necesitas fuerzas, puedes confiar en Él. Si quieres paz, Él te la puede dar. La mejor parte es que Dios honrará Su Palabra si le recuerdas sus promesas. En otras palabras, puedes descargar una aplicación para todas tus necesidades en la Palabra de Dios.

Ahora estoy mirándote . . .
A través de los ojos del amor

Cada persona tiene un propósito para estar aquí. Dios nos hizo únicos. En Su infinita sabiduría, El nos dio personalidades individuales, anhelos, dones y talentos especiales cuando Él nos creó.

Los talentos que Dios te dio para estar aquí son para que cumplas tu propósito. Tu trabajo es descubrir todos tus talentos para que los uses y para traerle gloria y honor. Después de todo, Él es quien te hizo. :) Y Él quiere que tú lo hagas sentirse orgulloso.

Vamos a hablar acerca de los dones y los talentos por un momento. Muchos talentos se desarrollan cuando los niños pasan de la etapa de niño hasta la etapa de la adolescencia. Es durante este tiempo que descubren la música (vocal e instrumental), las bellas artes, manualidades, carpintería y otras habilidades. Los niños aprenden desde una edad temprana si les gusta la música o el arte, la ciencia o las matemáticas, la comunicación o las artes escénicas.

A través de varios pasatiempos, puedes aprender a coser, tejer, tejer al croché, hacer modelos de carritos, o la carpintería. A la medida que maduras, otros intereses en las ciencias como medicina, odontología, ingeniería, comunicación masiva y todas formas de tecnología, periodismo, edición, etc. comenzarán a desarrollarse.

A la medida que recibes más exposición a nuevas ideas, nuevos conocimientos y nuevas oportunidades, lo más especializado y único serás en tu campo de interés. Se entiende que "los dones" que se desarrollan a niveles superiores de aprendizaje no son perseguidos o alcanzados hasta que uno alcance un cierto nivel de madurez (en la universidad o después).

Ahora, explicaré cómo el *bully* intercepta el propósito que Dios ha ordenado para tu vida.

¿Recuerdas el león cobarde del Mago de Oz? Él tenía miedo de todo y de todos. Él daba un salto de miedo cada vez que algo se movía a su alrededor. Sin embargo, ¿Él pasó todo su tiempo haciendo qué? Él asustaba a cualquiera que encontrara en su camino. Él no sólo era un cobarde, era un *bully*. ¿Entiendes ahora?

El *bully* es una distracción. El tiene una asignación: desviarte y hacerte perder la vista de tus sueños e impedirte que cumplas con tu propósito en la vida. Cuando te des cuenta que esto es lo que está pasando a través de las acciones del *bully*, podrás bailar alrededor de él/ella en el amor, como Muhammad Ali bailaba alrededor de sus oponentes antes de darles el golpe final.

Ahora, tú no vas a pelear con este *bully*, ni golpearlo, pero si ignoras sus tácticas y andas en el amor de

Cristo, él va a sentirse derrotado. Él verá que tú no estás afectado por sus acciones y será obvio a ellos que te observan que tú estás ganando este juego de El Quemado. :) ¿Dije yo **ganando**? Sí, ¡Tú eres un ganador! **¡Sí!**

Entonces sonríe y cuando sonrías, le causarás que pierda su enfoque en ti. ¡SONRÍE! **:)** Y sigue sonriendo. **:)**

Me Hizo Comprender

Me hizo comprender lo especial que soy.
Había algo que yo tenía
. . . algo que tú querías
. . . algo que tú necesitabas
. . . algo que encontraste en mi.

Había algo

En tu vida que te faltaba
. . . estabas mirando
. . . estabas buscando
. . . sólo necesitabas
"EL AMOR."

Querido Dios,

Te doy gracias por mis padres que siempre me han amado.
Yo oro que bendigas al *bully* para que encuentre en ti
El "amor" que el (ella) necesita tan desesperadamente.
Yo oro por aquellos menos afortunados, y que Tú
Suplas todas sus necesidades; pero sobre todo
Oro que Tú les bendigas y que les bendiga para siempre.

> > "Me estoy moviendo hacia adelante" > >

Moviendo hacia adelante===➔ ===➔ ===➔ ===➔ ===➔ ===➔ ===➔

¿A nadie le gusta la ropa que usas? *Crea tu propio estilo. Tal vez llegarás a ser el nombre más destacado en la industria de la moda.*

¿Ellos no te aceptan en su círculo de amigos? *No importa. Necesitas amigos verdaderos. Aprende a ser más selectivo. Tu tiempo es demasiado valioso para desperdiciarlo en personas que no quieren nada de la vida. Es beneficioso rodearte con personas más inteligentes que tú.*

¿Alguien habló mal de ti en Facebook? *Esto sí es difícil. ¿Cómo ignoras esto? Bueno, sólo tienes que elevarte por encima de ellos.*

Cada vez que estás ridiculizado o criticado abiertamente, las opiniones expresadas por lo general no tienen importancia tanto para ti como los motivos que están detrás de ellas. Caso en cuestión: No es tanto lo que la gente hace a nosotros lo que nos perjudica, es el motivo detrás de su acción lo que nos preocupa.

Si alguien habla desagradablemente sobre ti, si lo escuchas o no, te afecta por dentro. Si no se trata de inmediato, puede causar daño emocional. Atiéndelo de inmediato.

Se penetra en tu espíritu aun más cuando está en forma escrita, y peor si lo que dice no es cierto. Ese dolor se magnifica si el *bully* publica algo en Facebook® o Twitter® porque ahora es visible para que todo el mundo lo vea. Úsalo para tu ventaja.

Cuando respondas, escribe una comunicación abierta de perdón para que vean todos. Serás un ejemplo brillante.

Tu respuesta al mundo cibernético podría ser la siguiente:

"Los pasos que tomo hoy (cada día) son conectados directamente a mi futuro. Por eso, debo mantenerme enfocado en lograr mis metas. Así que, yo elijo perdonarte por las acciones que has tomado contra mi." *(Tu nombre)*

Al mantener tus principios altos, puedes elevarte por encima de los chismes y el ruido. El deseo de Dios para ti es una vida llena de bendiciones y favor cuando pones tu confianza en Él.

Siempre estés dispuesto a perdonar la persona que te ha lastimado, avergonzado, o humillado. El perdón es de vital importancia para sanarse sin dolor. Dios te respaldará, si lo pides. Él siempre se ocupa de ti.

"Echando toda vuestra ansiedad sobre él, porque él tiene cuidado de vosotros" (1 Pedro 5:7).
". . . Mía es la venganza, yo pagaré, dice el Señor" (Romanos 12:19b).

IX.

Tomando decisiones sabias

Tú eres una creación de Dios . . .

Tú eres una 'formidable y maravillosa creación'

Piensa en esto. ¡Qué maravillosa creación cuando Dios te hizo! No existe nadie exactamente igual a ti. Sólo hay uno como tú. Eso significa que tú eres único, excepcional, raro, y eso es bueno. ☺

Necesitarás lápiz y papel para esta sección. Ahora vamos a comenzar.

¿Que características/rasgos especiales te hacen único? Indirecta: ¿No puedes pensar en una? Aquí tienes una—tus huellas digitales.

Haz una lista de tres cosas que amas de ti. ¿Cuáles talentos/dones tienes? ¿Qué haces bien? ¿Cuáles son las "pequeñas cosas" que te hacen sentir feliz?

¿Que "pequeña cosa" puedes hacer por alguien para traerle gozo hoy? Indirecta: ¿Por qué no comienzas con tu familia (tu madre, padre, abuela/abuelo)? Cuando piensas en los demás y les tratas con amabilidad, tendrás menos tiempo para preocuparte por tus propios problemas.

Tu tarea #2: Contesta todas las preguntas en esta página. Comparte tus respuestas con tu madre y tu padre.

"Te alabaré; porque formidables, maravillosas son tus obras" (Salmos 139:14).

Tú estás aquí por una razón

Es importante que sepas que Dios te creó con un propósito. Naciste con ese propósito para llevarlo a cabo. Eres tan especial que nadie más puede hacerlo por ti. De hecho, eres insustituible.

Tú podrías ser el próximo gran científico, inventor o elaborador de producto. Hay algunos descubrimientos que todavía no han sido revelados, algunas innovaciones que todavía no han sido creadas, y misterios que necesitan ser resueltos. Hay productos que todavía tienen que ser elaborados y curas que necesitan ser encontradas.

¿Estás dispuesto a dejar que Dios haga grandes cosas por medio de ti? El mundo está esperando por tu contribución.

Ahora que tú entiendes que tienes un propósito para estar aquí, debes descubrir cuál es tu propósito. Si no estás seguro de lo que es, pregúntale a Dios: "¿Para qué fui creado? O pregúntale: "¿Cuál es mi propósito para estar aquí?"

Al instante que tú conozcas el propósito para lo cual tú naciste, sométete humildemente al plan de Dios para tu vida. No dejes que nada ni nadie te impida lograr el propósito que Dios te ha dado.

"Sé muy bien lo que tengo planeado para ustedes, dice el Señor, son planes para su bienestar, no para su mal. Son planes de darles un futuro y una esperanza" (Jeremías 29:11, NVI).

Tu decisión

Dios escucha cada vez que tú oras, pero Él es un Dios personal y un Padre amoroso. Él desea tener una relación personal contigo y una conversación "corazón a corazón" cada día.

Si tú nunca has recibido a Su Hijo, Jesús, como tu Señor y Salvador, el buen momento - el mejor momento – el tiempo correcto es ahora. Deja que Él haga una vida completamente nueva en ti.

Di esto en voz alta:

"Hoy pido ser perdonado por los pecados conocidos y los no conocidos. Padre Celestial, creo que tú enviaste a tu único Hijo, Jesucristo, a morir por mis pecados, que Él fue sepultado y resucitó al tercer día. Creo que su sangre derramada me limpia de toda maldad, y ahora soy justo delante de ti Padre, por tu sangre. Te acepto como mi Señor y Salvador personal, y ahora he vuelto a nacer".

Tú llegarás a conocer mejor a Dios si pasas tiempo leyendo Su palabra. Lo más tiempo que pases leyendo la Biblia, menos complicada será tu vida. Las repuestas a tus problemas se encuentran ahí.

Ahora, tú puedes despertarte feliz. Date a ti mismo la primera sonrisa cada día. Y piensa en cosas buenas.

Espera que el favor de Dios vaya delante de ti y que seas una bendición dondequiera que vayas. Espera recibir sus bendiciones en el camino.

Entrena tus pensamientos

Como un hombre piensa en su corazón, así es él. En otras palabras, somos lo que pensamos. Lo que pensamos es lo que decimos. Lo que hablamos y meditamos, es últimamente lo que llegamos a ser.

Sé consciente de tus pensamientos. Toma el control de ellos antes de que ellos tomen el control de ti. Sé consciente de lo que estás pensando en todo momento.

Poned la mirada en las cosas de arriba, no en las cosas de esta tierra. Esto significa que no te ocupes de las preocupaciones de este mundo.

Dios te ha preparado con la capacidad de hacer lo que te propongas hacer. Él puede fortalecerte para que hagas lo que normalmente sería imposible hacer.

Dios quitará el miedo a medida que se desarrolla tu fe. Entre más tiempo pases leyendo Su Palabra, más grande será tu fe. Entre más grande sea tu fe, más fuerte serás. Encontrarás que la fe en Dios anula todo temor, duda e incredulidad.

La felicidad es una decisión. Tu decides ser feliz, o no. Cuando tú comienzas a ser feliz, una sonrisa será fácil para ti.

Habla

A medida que comienzas a crecer más fuerte, verás el aumento en tu fe. Entonces, serás capaz de hablar de tu situación y hacer que la montana de la adversidad se desmorone a medida que la hablas.

Aquí hay algo que puedes decir:

"Yo elijo perdonar a aquellos que han venido en mi contra, tanto en el pasado como en el presente. No voy a guardar malos pensamientos y no mantendré ningún resentimiento en contra de ellos. Voy a ser fuerte y valiente, ya que estoy firme en la Palabra de Dios". Sepas que puedes tener lo que dices. Así que comienza a hablar las palabras que deseas tener.

Por ejemplo, tú puedes decir:

"Sé que Yo soy un ganador, y no se me ha dado un espíritu de temor, sino de poder, de amor y de dominio propio. Yo soy la cabeza, y no la cola; estaré encima solamente, y no estaré debajo. Me dirijo a la montaña de la adversidad para moverla fuera de mi camino, para lograr lo que yo he sido llamado y destinado a hacer. Yo, con éxito, alcanzaré mi propósito en la tierra, y nada se interpondrá en mi camino. Estoy muy emocionado acerca de la vida. Estoy muy emocionado con este día y lo que lograré. Padre, yo quiero honrarte con todo lo que digo y hago. Te doy las gracias por salvarme de toda forma de esclavitud, del

engaño, todas las mentiras, todo tipo de abuso verbal y físico, la angustia, la traición y la vergüenza. Gracias Señor por hacerme libre."

Conquistando al *bully*

Tú puedes conquistar al *bully* si tu:

- Ignoras a el/ella (si es posible)
- Mantienes tu distancia.
- Reemplazas el temor por la fe.
- Caminas en grupo, no solo.
- Buscas el consejo sabio.
- (Niños) Hablen con tus padres o con un adulto responsable.
- (Padres) Escuchen a tus hijos.

Puntos claves para recordar. **Consejos de supervivencias.**

▪ Conoce que tú eres una persona especial. Tu vida significa mucho para los miembros de tu familia y para tus amigos cercanos porque sólo hay uno como tú. Sé selectivo a quien tú das tu tiempo, atención y talentos.

▪ Mantente lejos de los agitadores. No pongas atención a los comentarios crueles que ellos dicen. Mantente mirando hacia arriba y moviéndote hacia delante.

▪ Si tú has sido atacado por un *bully*, no es recomendable que tú también pelees. Sin embargo, es importante que lo reportes inmediatamente. No estarías recibiendo ayuda sólo para ti. Tu acción podría ayudar que el *bully* reciba la atención que él o ella necesita también.

▪ Mantén a tus padres o los adultos responsables de ti informados acerca de cada incidente cada vez que seas

atacado. Habla con ellos. Perdona a la persona que te atacó. Y sigue hablando con tus padres/familia/ tus seres queridos hasta que te sientas mejor.

▪ Reemplaza el dolor (de ser avergonzado o humillado) con pensamientos positivos, actividades y obras amables. Trata de no pensar sólo en ti mismo, es decir, debes buscar a otros niños que han sido *bullied* como tú y ofrecerle tu apoyo.

▪ Si estás siendo *bullied* en camino a la escuela, puedes considerar ir acompañado o tomar una ruta diferente. Trata de estar rodeado, cuanto sea posible, con personas que de corazón quieren tu bienestar.

▪ No permitas que las distracciones te impidan lograr tu propósito en la vida. Vive cada día para el futuro porque tu futuro es brillante.

▪ Para evitar distracciones, mantén tus pensamientos por encima de los chismes.

▪ Recuerda: siempre haz lo mejor, sé lo mejor, espera lo mejor. Mantén una actitud positiva todo el tiempo.

▪ Sonríe desde adentro hacia afuera. Una sonrisa puede marcar la diferencia en los resultados.

▪ Aprende a esquivar la pelota y diviértete al hacerlo. Juega el juego de esquivar la pelota y gana.

▪ El verdadero campeón es quien sabe cómo ignorar al enemigo. No trates de ganar cada batalla por ti mismo. Deja que Dios pelee por ti. Usa las armas espirituales que Él te ha dado.

- Deja que la paz comience contigo. Sé amable contigo mismo y con los demás.

Tu tarea #3: Busca información en el internet acerca de la poderosa águila o lee un libro en la librería. Estudia sus características y escríbelas en un papel.

X.

Madres y padres cariñosos

Las madres y los padres cariñosos

Esta sección es para ti =======

```
                                  |
                                  |
                                  |
                                  |
                                  |
                              \\  |  //
                               \\|//
                                \|/
```

Los niños son el bien más preciado de la institución - la familia.

¿Qué se ha perdido?

Hay cinco ingredientes claves que están perdidos en muchos hogares. Están enlistados más abajo.

"Amor"
La "ausencia del amor" viene de los padres que no son capaces de amarse a ellos mismos por causa de sus experiencias pasadas. Amarte a ti mismo es un prerrequisito para amar a tu hijo incondicionalmente. Con el amor viene la amabilidad. Cuando eres amable contigo mismo, es más fácil mostrar amabilidad a otros.

"Una demostración de amor"
Es importante decir "Te amo" a tus hijos, pero igualmente como importante es la demostración de tu amor en tus acciones, obras, palabras, y el tono de voz.

"Buena comunicación"
Es buena cosa hablar con tus hijos respetuosamente porque ellos aprenden de tu ejemplo. Siempre comparta información importante con ellos y anímelos a hacer lo mismo.

"Buenas habilidades para escuchar"
Cuando uno de tus hijos comience a compartir, escucha. "Escucha" aun si lo que tu hijo dice te duele un poco. Necesitas saber lo que ellos están pensando.

"La oración"
Las palabras no pueden explicar la importancia de este ingrediente. Este ingrediente no sólo puede unir la familia, sino una nación si el pueblo se pusiera de acuerdo. Comienza cada día con la oración. Ora constantemente. También, ora por los demás.

Usando la autoridad dada por Dios

El ciberespacio: Atacando la actividad.

Los niños (y los adolescentes también) necesitan saber y estar seguros del amor de sus padres, y que con el amor viene la disciplina, la orientación y un conjunto de reglas para vivir. Hay que enseñarles a honrar, respetar y obedecer la autoridad.

La buena comunicación es vital para establecer y mantener un ambiente familiar sano y cariñoso dentro de la familia. Así que Mamá y Papá, es tiempo de volver a lo básico.

Como padres, ustedes experimentarán muchas recompensas si sientan las bases, y trabajan para mantener un diálogo abierto entre ustedes y sus hijos. Es importante que ellos se sientan cómodos al hablar con ustedes de sus problemas.

Tú eres la autoridad en la casa, y tú tendrás que tomar control de las actividades en la computadora de la casa, aun si tienes que restringir las horas en el internet, apagarla durante un tiempo, o restringir el uso del teléfono celular, etc.

Depende de ti ejercer tu autoridad dada por Dios en todo momento. También es importante que tú puedas controlar la duración del tiempo en el internet y supervisar la actividad cibernética en tu casa.

Después de haber establecido algunas reglas básicas, anima a tus hijos a usar el internet con prudencia, es decir, fines educativos. Muéstrales cómo estas y otras actividades familiares realizadas en la computadora

pueden ser a su beneficio. Deje que los medios de comunicación social también sean una actividad familiar.

Tú puedes utilizar el internet como fuente para extraer información valiosa y encontrar formas creativas para que sea una experiencia divertida (no te olvides de los juegos que se pueden jugar en la computadora).

La computadora también se puede utilizar para la investigación y el conocimiento. Muchos estudiantes universitarios al terminar sus estudios se dan cuenta luego que eligieron la carrera equivocada. ¿Por qué no ayudas a tus hijos a investigar varias carreras antes de ir a la universidad?

A través de la investigación, muchas carreras han florecidas, muchos descubrimientos se han hecho, y muchas curas han sido encontradas. Y a través de la investigación, puede mejorar su vida y la vida de los demás.

Tarea #4: ¿Por qué no empiezas hoy? Haz que tus hijos investiguen los temas relacionados con sus intereses. Aprendan juntos y deje que sea una experiencia gratificante. En esta tarea, tus hijos aprenderán la importancia de ser diligente.

"¿Has visto hombre solícito en su trabajo? Delante de los reyes estará; No estará delante de los de baja condición." (Proverbios 22:29).

Buscando respuestas

(En todos los lugares correctos)

La Palabra de Dios dice que tenemos que entrenar a un niño en el camino que debe seguir, y cuando ese niño sea viejo no se apartará de el. Para entrenar a un niño en el camino de Dios, debes ser un ejemplo y enseñarle cómo usar la Biblia como guía para su vida diaria.

Al hacerlo, tú vives la vida que Él desea que tengas, una vida llena de fe, llena de las bendiciones y el favor de Dios; dominando el mal. No hay nada más poderoso que la palabra hablada.

Padres, si no están enseñando a sus niños la Palabra de Dios, comiencen hoy. Hay protección, seguridad, consuelo, sanidad, vida, sabiduría, paz, gozo, poder, amor, refugio y fortaleza en la Palabra de Dios.

Tus hijos necesitan todo esto para defenderse del *bully* y otras fuerzas del mal. Sé el ejemplo y ellos seguirán tu ejemplo.

Tarea #5: Asegúrate de armar a tus hijos con la Palabra de Dios. Funciona como una espada contra los malhechores. Tus hijos pueden escribir los versículos de la Biblia en tarjetas 3 x 5. Esta forma les ayudará a memorizar más fácil la Palabra de Dios. Por favor toma en cuenta los versículos de la Biblia en la página 104.

Guía para los padres:

Queridos Mamás y Papás,

Los niños que son enseñados en El Señor disfrutan de gran paz. En esta sección del libro, voy a compartir algunos versículos de la Biblia que les darán vida, sanación, y crecimiento a ti y a tus hijos.

En primer lugar, instruyan a sus hijos en la importancia de sus palabras y compartan lo siguiente con ellos: Tus palabras - las palabras que tú hablas - trabajarán a tu favor o en tu contra.

Enseña a tu hijo a hablar palabras de vida, porque *"La muerte y la vida están en poder de la lengua, y él que la ama comerá de sus frutos"* (Proverbios 18:21). Las palabras que decimos deben dar vida a nosotros. Elige sus palabras sabiamente.

Estos versículos de la Biblia construirán la fe y aumentarán la resistencia a cualquier problema que pueda surgir en el camino de tu hijo. A modo que estas palabras de vida sean aplicadas a sus vidas, ellos vendrán a conocer y disfrutar de la paz de Dios que sobrepasa todo entendimiento.

"Jehová está conmigo; no temeré lo que me pueda hacer el hombre". (Salmos 118:6)

"Ninguna arma forjada contra ti prosperará..." (Isaías 54:17).

"... Si Dios es por nosotros (mi), ¿Quién contra nosotros (mi)?" (Romanos 8:31).

"Antes, en todas estas cosas somos (soy) más que vencedores por medio de aquel que nos amó" (Romanos 8:37).

"Todo lo puedo en Cristo que me fortalece" (Filipenses 4:13).

Tomando la autoridad a través de la oración

Amados Padres,

Caminar en el amor de Cristo comienza en el hogar. ¿Les dices a tus hijos que los amas? ¿Les aseguras de tu amor todos los días?

Aunque no puedes estar con tus hijos para protegerlos en cada momento del día, hay algo que puedes hacer. Tú puedes hacer que tus hijos sean "a prueba de bully" a través de la oración y las confesiones de La Palabra cada día. La oración en la página siguiente, si la incorporan a la vida cotidiana de tu hijo, producirá cambios positivos para toda la vida.

Las palabras de vida que ellos dicen aumentarán su fe en el Dios amoroso y desarrollarán su confianza en Su Palabra. Les ayudarán salir victorioso en cada área de tus vidas.

Esta oración es positivamente buena. Toda la familia puede usarla. Tú y tus hijos sabrán que pueden hacer cualquier cosa que están determinados hacer con la ayuda de Dios porque Él ha prometido fortalecerles en el camino.

Nota para los Padres: Si tú no has recibido a Jesús como Señor y Salvador en su vida, yo te extiendo una invitación hoy. La oración de salvación se encuentra en la pagina 90.

Dé a sus hijos un abrazo cada día.

Haz tu hijo "a prueba de bully" a través de la oración

(Con palabras de vida)

Enseña a tus hijos que Dios es Omnisciente, Omnipotente, y Omnipresente. Dios sabe todas las cosas, es Todopoderoso, y está en cada lugar todo el tiempo.

Anima a tu hijo que diga la siguiente oración al inicio de cada día para activar la protección y el favor de Dios en la vida de él/ella.

La Oración de ____________________________:

(El nombre de tu hijo va aquí)

"Buenos días Dios. Hoy será un gran día si Tú me acompañas. Gracias por los ángeles que has puesto a mi alrededor para que me protejan y me mantengan a salvo.

Creo que Tu Palabra, que yo hablo, se cumplirán.

Estoy muy agradecido de que Tú te encargarás de cualquier persona que venga en mi contra, porque Tú dices que la venganza te pertenece. Eso significa que nunca tendré que luchar. Creo en la promesa que dice, que Tú harás que hasta mis enemigos estén en paz conmigo.

Sé que nunca me dejarás, ni nunca me abandonarás. Gracias Dios porque cada vez que te necesite, siempre estarás ahí para mí.

Estaré en tu presencia todo el día porque en tu presencia hay plenitud de gozo. Gracias por mantenerme en perfecta paz.

Dios, te amo. Gracias por cuidarme y preocuparte tanto por mí. Esta es mi oración en el nombre de Jesús. Amen."

Haz tu hijo "a prueba de bully" con palabras de vida

Utilice la siguiente confesión para aumentar la fe de tu hijo en un Dios amoroso, para construir un muro de protección alrededor de su corazón y sus emociones, y para darle la certeza de la presencia de Dios en todo momento. Hazle saber que no hay necesidad de temer porque Dios está presente y vive en su corazón.

La confesión de __________:(Dila todos los días)
(Nombre de tu hijo)

"Dios dice que soy hecho formidable y maravilloso. Yo soy la cabeza y no la cola. Yo estoy por encima solamente y no por debajo. Y yo soy el principio, y no el último."

Creo que la Palabra de Dios dice que: "Ninguna arma forjada en contra mí prosperará, ni me va a causar ningún daño. Dios es mi refugio y fortaleza, nuestro pronto auxilio en las tribulaciones.

Elijo pensar en las cosas buenas, hacer buenas obras y compartir buenas noticias. Voy a hacer una diferencia positiva en las personas cuyas vidas toco. Quiero impactar el mundo con el bien.

Hoy voy a encontrar cosas de que reírme y mantener el corazón contento porque la risa es como una medicina (para mí). Me hace bien.

Tarea #6: Haz que tu hijo confiese afirmaciones positivas cada día. La anterior es una gran manera de comenzar. Nota: Al hacer esta actividad, hará que tu hijo crezca y se fortalezca en todos los ámbitos de la

vida, al igual que el atleta que tiene un régimen diario de acondicionamiento y entrenamiento de resistencia.

Índice de las Escrituras para Oraciones pág.107:

Dios ordenará que sus ángeles te cuiden en todos tus caminos. {Lee Salmo 91:11}.
"La Palabra de Dios no retornará a Él vacías..." {Lee Isaías 55:11}.
"La venganza es mía; dice el Señor Yo pagaré" {Romanos 12:19}.
...Cuando el Señor aprueba la conducta de un hombre, hasta con sus enemigos lo reconcilia – {Lee Proverbios 16:7}.
Dios dice, "Nunca te dejaré; jamás te abandonaré" – {Hebreos 13:5}.
"En su presencia hay plenitud de gozo"{Lee Salmo 16:11}.
Al de carácter firme lo guardarás en perfecta paz, porque en ti confía – {Isaías 26:3}.
Él cuida de ustedes- {Lee 1 Pedro 5:7}.

Índice de las Escrituras para Confesiones pág.109:

"...Soy una creación admirable; tus obras son maravillosas..."'{ Salmo 139:14}.
"...El Señor te pondrá a la cabeza, nunca en la cola; Siempre estarás en la cima, nunca en el fondo;..."{ Lee Deuteronomio 28:13}.
"Ninguna arma forjada contra tí prevalecerá..."{Isaías 54:17}.
"Dios es nuestro {mi} amparo y fortaleza, nuestra ayuda segura en momentos de angustia." {Salmo 46:1}.
"Consideren bien todo lo verdadero, todo lo puro, todo lo amable, todo lo digno de admiración, en fin, todo lo que sea excelente o merezca elogio. . .{Lee Filipenses 4:8}.
"Gran remedio es el corazón alegre..." {Proverbios 17:22}.

XI.

Sólo para **los *bullies***

Esta sección es

Sólo para los *bullies*:

Es posible que hayas estado pensando de qué trata este libro. El siguiente segmento fue creado sólo para ti.

¿Quién te controla?

Todo el mundo tiene adversidad o ha sufrido de algún tipo de aflicción. Todos han experimentado la desilusión o la tristeza en su vida. El trabajo del enemigo es mantenerte desanimado durante los momentos difíciles. Si estás experimentando adversidad, escala esa montaña paso a paso y confía en Dios.

¿Sabes quién es el enemigo? Sólo hay un enemigo – Satanás – que manipula la mente de la gente para hacer maldad. El enemigo viene para robar, matar, y destruir.

El comediante, Flip Wilson, hizo este concepto fácil para entender. Algunos de tus padres pueden recordar a Flip Wilson. Cada vez que él interpretaba un personaje especial e hizo algo que no debería hacer, él sonreía tímidamente y decía, "El diablo me hizo hacerlo."

Él tenía toda la razón, porque Dios nunca te dirá que hagas nada malo. Dios es bueno y sólo hace lo bueno. El te ama tanto y no va a invocar mal sobre ti.

"El ladrón no viene sino para hurtar, matar y destruir; yo he venido para que tengan vida, y para que la tengan en abundancia" (Juan 10:10).

Tienes que decidir:

¿Eres un pollo, cangrejo, o águila?

Oye *Bully*,

Es hora que tú decidas. Has pasado mucho tiempo haciendo la vida miserable a otras personas y probablemente ni sabes por qué. Me gustaría ponerte a pensar en algo. Aquí está mi cuento acerca de los pollos, los cangrejos, y las águilas.

Primeramente, es importante que conozcas cada animal y cómo se relaciona con las características humanas. Al leer acerca de ellos, puedes tomar una decisión sobre tu futuro.

En este ejemplo:

"Los Pollos" – Por lo general, representan las personas que falta dirección en su vida porque no saben lo que quieren hacer con su vida, ni hacia dónde se dirigen.

"Los Cangrejos" – Son las personas que tratan de detener tu éxito.

"Las Águilas"– Son nuestros líderes, inspiradores y personajes influyentes. Son los grandes y honorables soldados. Son aquellos que saben y disfrutan de servir a los demás sin condiciones. Son personas comunes y corrientes que hacen cosas extraordinarias. Son aquellos que usan todos sus talentos y dones dados por Dios.

La vida está llena de pollos, cangrejos, y águilas. ¿Cuál eres tú?

Ahora explicaré cómo trabaja cada uno en sus pequeños círculos de influencia:

Los pollos andan picoteando de ida y vuelta sin rumbo nunca alejándose del gallinero. Los cangrejos, al otro lado, cuando están guardados en un barril se aseguran que el otro nunca salga.

El águila – se describe como raro, fuerte, único, poderoso - es impulsado por el éxito. Las águilas son conocidas y admiradas por su fuerza. Las águilas vuelan alto. Vuelan tan alto que los cuervos que les gusta molestar constantemente no pueden alcanzarlas.

¿No preferirías ser un águila? Para ser un águila, debes cambiar la dirección de tus viajes y trazar un nuevo curso. Tendrás que elevarte por encima de la mentalidad del gallinero y salir del barril.

Tú, mi amigo(a), puedes cambiar la dirección de tu actitud. Para cambiar tu actitud, puedes levantar la altitud de tu mente y elevar tus pensamientos.

A la medida que aprendas amarte a ti mismo, podrás amar a tu prójimo. Al comenzar a ver el mundo a través de los ojos del amor, tu vida tomará nuevo significado. Las cosas se convertirán frescas y nuevas, y lo viejo pasará.

Tú puedes volar como el águila. . . porque eres una persona especial.

Tu tarea: Estudia los hábitos y características de la poderosa águila. ¿No sería mejor ser un águila?

Más pensamientos

(El acto de *bullying* crea una línea fina entre la vida y la muerte.)

Los *bullies* no se dan cuenta de que sus acciones podrían contribuir a una fatalidad. En una entrevista que presentó el programa *Today Show* de MSNBC, el *bully* tenía mucho remordimiento por las acciones que había tomado en contra de la víctima que se suicidó.

Pero ya era demasiado tarde para la víctima que había sufrido más de tres (3) meses de insultos, comentarios degradantes por el internet, y amenazas de agresión física. Fue demasiado para soportar.

Y ahora es demasiado tarde para aquellos que son acusados por conducta criminal y asalto porque el daño ya está hecho. No tiene que ser así para ti.

¿De verdad quieres desperdiciar tu vida, tu reputación, y tu futuro prometedor? ¿Vale ser un *bully* y ser encarcelado el resto de la vida?

No esperes hasta que sea demasiado tarde. Detén el bullying ahora. Puedes cambiar tu vida hoy. La decisión es tuya.

Tu decisión

(Da tu corazón a Dios)

Dios te escucha cada vez que oras porque Él es un Dios personal y un Padre amoroso. Su deseo es tener una relación personal contigo y comunicarse contigo "corazón a corazón" diariamente.

Si no has recibido a Jesucristo como tu Señor y Salvador personal, un buen momento – el mejor momento – es hacerlo ahora mismo. Necesitas que Él esté en tu vida hoy. Déjalo hacer de tu vida una vida nueva.

Di en voz alta: "Padre Celestial, yo vengo a ti en el nombre de Jesucristo. Por favor, perdóname por ser antipático con otros. Perdóname por ser un *bully* y por lastimar a personas inocentes. Yo creo que Tú puedes sanarme de toda forma de abuso, dolor, angustia, decepción, rechazo, y el miedo de ser rechazado. Yo quiero mejorar mi vida y cambiar mi forma de pensar. Estoy listo para cambiar mi vida por la vida mejor que tienes para mi."

Ora en voz alta:

"Señor, yo creo que enviaste a Tu Hijo unigénito, Jesucristo, para morir en la cruz por mis pecados, y que Él fue sepultado en la tumba y resucitó al tercer día. Creo que su sangre derramada me limpia de toda maldad, y ahora soy justo delante del Padre. Yo te acepto como mi Señor y Salvador personal, y ahora mismo he nacido de nuevo."

¡Felicidades! Este es un día muy especial para ti. Anota este día y celebra tu día de nuevos comienzos

cada año. Celebramos la decisión más importante de tu vida.

No es tan complicado

La Palabra de Dios puede cambiar tus pensamientos, palabras y acciones.

La mente siempre está ocupada con pensamientos. Algunos pensamientos son buenos y otros no tan buenos. Con el tiempo te convertirás en lo que piensas y en lo que dices. Tu mente tiene mucho que ver con eso.

Hay una atracción natural del hombre para hacer el mal debido a la naturaleza pecaminosa del primer hombre, Adán. Por lo tanto, hay que aprovechar cada oportunidad para llenar la mente con pensamientos positivos, afirmaciones positivas, y promesas maravillosas para combatir la naturaleza pecaminosa.

Lo que pensamos, sentimos y lo que decimos está controlado por la actividad del cerebro - la mente. Si tienes un gran día o un día no tan maravilloso, la mente tiene algo que ver con esto.

Si estás pensando constantemente en pensamientos de celos, expresarás sentimientos de envidia a través de tus acciones. Si estás enojado, expresarás enojo. Un hombre o mujer enojada nunca está en un estado de tranquilidad. Si estás molesto o inquieto, molestarás aquellos a tu alrededor y causarás un estado de inquietud dondequiera que vayas.

Lo positivo es que tú puedes, a propósito, cambiar tu forma de pensar para mejorar la calidad de tu vida. Al pasar más tiempo en la Palabra de Dios, puedes hacer un esfuerzo consciente para vivir una vida más productiva. De hecho, la vida será menos complicada

cuando refresques la mente diariamente con las maravillosas Palabras de Vida.

XII.

Preocúpate lo suficiente como para compartir

Mostrando que te preocupas lo suficiente como para compartir

Si podrías salvar la vida de un niño al compartir este libro, ¿Lo harías?

Demasiadas vidas se han perdido ya, porque los padres y los niños no fueron informados. Vamos a ser proactivos en la prevención del *bully*. Vamos a trabajar juntos para preservar nuestras futuras generaciones.

Quizás tú conoces a un niño o adolescente que podría beneficiarse de la información proporcionada en este libro. Al compartir esta información, ayudarás a preservar lo sagrado de la vida.

Si elegiste este libro por casualidad, te animo a que lo comparta. Compra una copia adicional para otra persona, o considera regalar este mismo libro porque te preocupas lo suficiente para compartir.

Lectura recomendada: "Cómo Superar Todos Los Obstáculos... Y Aterrizar En La Cima" de Patrice Lee.

http://behavioral-management.com/bullying-statistics (Marzo 28, 2011)

Kids Who Bully Are Twice As Likely To Have Sleep Problems, Study Finds. [Los niños que intimidan son dos veces más propensos a tener trastornos del sueño, según estudio.] *Michigan Chronicle, Health. Junio 8-14, 2011.*

La Palabra de Dios: La Biblia

Bully me?. . . Preguntas de repaso

1. La mayoría de los *bullies* son infelices. F/V

2. El ataque de un *bully* no es más que una expresión de dolor del pasado, ira o decepción. F/V

3. Nombra tres lugares donde puedes ir en busca de ayuda si has sido *bullied.*

4. Si te conviertes en una victima de un *bully*, ¿Qué es lo primero que debes hacer?

5. Nombra siete armas de manera no violentas que puedes usar en contra de los ataques del *bully.*

6. Menciona tres características acerca de ti que te hacen maravillosamente único. (Está bien que se jactes aquí) ☺

7. ¿Cuál es el mejor regalo espiritual que puedes poner en acción? (Indirecta: El amor nunca falla).

8. ¿Cuáles son las cuatro cosas que puedes hacer para ayudarte a mirar a través de los ojos del amor?

9. Nombra cuatro tipos de *bullies.*

10. ¿Qué puedes hacer para ayudar a alguien que haya sido *bullied*?

11. ¿Cómo puedes mostrar apoyo a otros que necesitan ayuda?

12. ¿Puedes explicar cómo aplicar la teoría del juego "El Quemado", si confrontas a un *bully* en el salón de clases o un jefe que es *bully*?

13. ¿Cómo puedes usar el internet como una herramienta para mejorar tu futuro?

14. Dejar que la paz comience contigo es un buen hábito que debes practicar. F/V

15. ¿Qué puedes hacer en la escuela o en el vecindario para detener al *bully*? Tú puedes marcar la diferencia.

16. Dentro de cincuenta palabras o menos, dinos que puedes hacer para marcar una diferencia positiva en el mundo.

17. ¿Cómo puedes influir en tus compañeros para que hagan cambios positivos en sus vidas?

18. ¿Qué planeas lograr en los próximos 6 meses, 12 meses? Escribe tus metas. Sé específico. Explica cómo vas a ejecutar tu plan.

19. ¿Cuáles son tus metas para los próximos 5 años? Escríbelas. Haz una lista de los pasos que tomarás para lograr estas metas.

Actividad para la familia:

20. Hagan un tablero de la visión familiar. Pueden usar fotos, palabras, o el texto de los periódicos. Necesitarán pegamento y tijeras para empezar. Sean creativos. Al terminar el tablero de la visión, manténganlo en un lugar visible, y revísenlo diariamente hasta que hayan cumplido sus metas.

Aquí hay algunas ideas para ayudarte y a tu hijo a comenzar:

a. Tu hijo(a) puede diseñar un tablero de su visión según lo que quiere lograr durante el año escolar.
b. Si tu hijo(a) tiene la edad suficiente para trabajar tiempo parcial y de ir a la escuela, él (ella) puede mostrar lo que va a hacer con su dinero o mostrar las cosas que quiere comprar con sus ingresos.
c. Otro niño puede crear un tablero con la visión de sus futuras metas profesionales.
d. Los abuelos pueden hacer tableros con sus visiones también. Si tus abuelos están enfermos, han sufrido una lesión, o están incapacitados temporalmente, tú puedes ayudarles hacer un tablero de visión que muestre a personas de todas las edades caminando con gusto. ¿Entiendes la idea?

21. Cuando hayan logrado todo en su tablero de visión, hagan uno nuevo.

22. Acuérdate: Los brazos del *bully* son demasiados cortos para pelear con Dios. **:)**

NO MÁS BULLYING! ! !

Para comprar más libros visita:

www.ucantbullyme.com

Patrice Lee continua escribir y publicar libros. Ella está disponible para hablar a las empresas, grupos de jóvenes de la iglesia, conferencias, seminarios, a estudiantes de las escuelas primarias y escuelas secundarias y Asociaciones de Madres y Padres.

Si este libro te ha ayudado en cualquier forma, infórmanos. Estaremos felices de recibir tus comentarios a: ucantbullyme@gmail.com

Más libros por Patrice Lee:

Bully Me? . . .Oh NO!!! (para los adolescentes)
*"...**Overcome Every Obstacle** and Land on Top"*
"Happy To Be ME" (para los niños pequeños)
"My Dad, My Friend" (para los niños pequeños)

www.ingramcontent.com/pod-product-compliance
Lightning Source LLC
Chambersburg PA
CBHW050558300426
44112CB00013B/1972
9780983720713

www.ingramcontent.com/pod-product-compliance
Lightning Source LLC
Chambersburg PA
CBHW050558300426
44112CB00013B/1971

* 9 7 8 0 9 8 7 1 1 5 1 0 2 *